Redux

Redux

Designs That Reuse, Recycle, and Reveal

Jennifer Roberts

Gibbs Smith, Publisher
Salt Lake City

First Edition

09 08 07 06 05 5 4 3 2 1

Published by

Gibbs Smith, Publisher

P.O. Box 667

Layton, Utah 84041

Orders: 1.800.748.5439

www.gibbs-smith.com

Designed by John T. Nuttall, Richards & Swensen Graphic Design

Printed and bound in Hong Kong

Library of Congress Cataloging-in-Publication Data

Roberts, Jennifer, 1962-

Redux : designs that reuse, recycle, and reveal/ Jennifer Roberts.—1st ed.

p. cm.

ISBN 1-58685-701-0

1. Architecture—Environmental aspects. 2. Architecture, Domestic—United States. I. Title.

NA2542.35.R645 2005

728'.37—dc22

2005012297

"The dump was our poetry and our history. We took it home with us by the wagonload, bringing back into town the things the town had used and thrown away."

—Wallace Stegner, "The Town Dump"

Contents

NEW CONSTRUCTION

Introduction

What's Inside

This is a book of stories about homes that look great and do good. Each chapter tells the tale of a beautifully crafted home and the people who created it. Alongside the main narratives are shorter accounts of connected ideas, people and places, as well as practical tips and helpful resources.

At first glance the featured homes may seem quite different from one another, but at heart they share these traits:

❑ *They reuse and recycle old buildings and old stuff.* The homes span the spectrum of reuse, from places where the recycling story is behind the walls to homes that wear their salvage on their sleeves. A number are eco-sensitive renovations of old or not-so-old houses. Some are green adaptations of buildings or other structures not originally intended to house people. Still others are brand-new homes built with reused materials, from salvaged airplane flaps to discarded billboards.

❏ *They're green.* In varying degrees, or shades of green, these homes were built or remodeled to be healthier to live in, easier on the environment, more energy efficient and comfortable, and longer lasting than conventionally built homes.

❏ *They embody the beauty and diversity of ecological design.* For some people, words like *salvaged* or *reused* connote damaged goods, and labels like *ecological design* stir up visions of drearily earnest dwellings. But have no fear— the homes in these pages engage our senses; they draw us in with their good looks long before we grasp that their beauty is more than skin deep. Granted, not every home in this book may be to your taste, but that's part of the point: today's ecological design is diverse, covering the spectrum from cutting edge to traditional, from subtle to in-your-face, from city apartments to suburban dwellings to rural retreats.

Rewards of Reuse

Reusing time-worn buildings and building materials is often more satisfying than the immediate gratification of buying a pristine new thing. Here are some reasons why:

❏ *Individuality.* The dominance of chain stores and the Internet means that today a Tampa resident can dash into Pottery Barn (or just go online) and furnish her dining room with the same table, chairs and even napkin rings as her cousin in Tacoma. To be sure, conformity has its comforts and conveniences, but why shouldn't our homes be as individual as we are? In these pages you'll see a plethora of one-of-a-kind homes and details, from countertops hewn from storm-felled trees to trellises built of salvaged steel railroad tracks.

© 2005 Laurie Lambrecht

❏ *Quality.* If something has lasted long enough to make it worth reusing, it was likely well made or of superior quality in the first place — possibly of much higher quality than a new product we'd buy at our local big-box retailer. This is especially true of antique wood that's recovered from abandoned factories, barns, river bottoms and old homes and is prized for its strength, character, stability, and in many cases, sheer size. New lumber, on the other hand, is mostly milled from fast-growing, small-diameter trees harvested from farms or second- or third-growth forests; it rarely holds a candle to salvaged timbers hewn a hundred years ago from centuries-old trees.

❏ *Beauty.* Maybe it's middle age creeping up on me (okay, staring back at me in the mirror), but I have a bias toward faces etched with laugh lines, kitchen tables that show the wear and tear of countless meals, and houses built from

© 2005 Randi Baird

stuff that's been around the block a few times. Beauty is a slippery concept to bat around. Nothing's more subjective, after all. But as you'll see, whether it's cargo containers transformed into a contemporary home or a nineteenth-century icehouse converted into apartments, old materials and old buildings reused in new and eco-friendly ways can take the breath away.

❏ *Visibility.* Most green building products and techniques won't make your home look any different than their conventional counterparts. This unobtrusiveness has its advantages and disadvantages. It helps increase acceptance because being green no longer means that a house has to look eccentric. But if you've gone to the trouble of making your home more eco-friendly, haven't you earned some bragging rights? This is another of reuse's strong suits. Your friends' eyes may glaze over when you talk about the high R-value of your wall insulation, but show them your kitchen floor of salvaged slate roof tiles, and they may well turn green with envy.

❏ *Romance of the past.* We admire things that have withstood the test of time — cobblestones recovered when a city street is torn up, rough-hewn timbers reclaimed when a textile mill is torn down. And we love stories about the things that make our house a home, in part because these stories connect us to other times, people and places. They help us make sense of who we are. I live in San Francisco, near the old shipyards, in a house built in the early 1890s. When the previous owners renovated the house forty years ago, they installed in the front hall two large pendant lamps made of rosewood, bronze and glass. Those lamps once hung in the reception area of an old SPCA building a mile and a half from here, but were taken out when the building was modernized. A few years after buying our house, we went over to the same SPCA and brought home another recycled treasure, a big-eared mutt named Moxie. It's just a slight connection, not likely to resonate deeply with others, and yet, knowing where those lamps came from and feeling a tie to that history gives me great delight and a real sense of belonging to this place.

❏ *A helping hand for the planet.* Using something old is often easier on the environment than buying new. Reuse reduces pressure to extract or mine nonrenewable resources from the earth or to harvest slow-growing renewable resources like redwoods. According to the Rainforest Alliance, an international conservation group, a dismantled warehouse with one million board feet of reusable lumber can offset the need to harvest one thousand acres of forest. There are exceptions, of course, to the old-is-better-than-new rule. If you have antique barn timbers shipped from southern France to your construction site in Idaho, you're using a lot of energy getting them from there to here. In that case, new timbers from a sustainably managed forest in the Pacific Northwest might make more sense. Reuse is often good for the environment, but not always, so take care to weigh the pros and cons of old versus new.

Why Reuse Matters (My Trash Is Your Trash)

Renovating older buildings is hardly revolutionary. And reusing salvaged or recycled materials when remodeling a home or building a new one isn't groundbreaking news.

So why a book about reusing old stuff and old buildings? Why now?

❏ Because a 300-year-old redwood, once cut down, is gone for good.

❏ Because we're bulldozing houses before they've outlived their first mortgages and we're burying the stuff they're made of in holes in the ground.

❏ Because some of the new goods we use to build or remodel our homes are of questionable quality at best and poisonous at worst.

© 2005 J. D. Peterson

Our efforts to achieve the good life for ourselves and our families are having unintended consequences on the planet. Ancient trees, fisheries, fossil fuels, fresh water, wildlands — they're going fast. Most scientists now believe that even the global climate is changing as a consequence of how we design, make and use things.

Others have said it before me: we are merely borrowing this land from our children. We have an obligation to return it to them healthier and stronger than when it was temporarily put in our care.

Fortunately there are countless steps we can take in our everyday lives to nudge the environment toward healthier conditions. Many of these steps hinge on the home-design choices we make, whether we're sprucing up a room, remodeling our home or taking the plunge into building the house of our dreams.

Slow Food and Delicious Homes

© 2005 Eric Laignel

Looking back over the homes I've included here, I'm reminded of the slow-food movement that's flourishing in Italy and other parts of the world, including the United States — the birthplace of fast food. Slow food means preparing delicious, satisfying meals using nutritious, locally grown ingredients. It celebrates the pleasures of the table and traditional values like sharing a meal and conversation with family and friends.

Slow food takes more time and often costs more money than grabbing a bag of burgers at McDonald's. But the rewards are bountiful: self-reliance, health, biodiversity, creativity, beauty, stronger connections with family and community.

My point? The homes in this book were created by people with that slow-food spirit; they are lovingly crafted places designed with respect and built with wholesome, quality materials. These are delicious homes.

In the course of writing this book, I've met dozens of homeowners, architects, builders and craftspeople. I've been struck not only by how mindful these folks are of the effects of their actions on the environment but also by how modestly they talk about their accomplishments. None of them made grand claims about saving the planet or revolutionizing home design. Instead they point to incremental steps and small wins: persuading a client to remodel instead of tear down, getting the local building department to accept an improved method of building with straw bales, tracking down a concrete supplier who will add recycled fly ash to the mix.

Small steps, maybe, but they're headed in the right direction, and that can add up to major change.

Is Reuse Worth the Trouble? (It Isn't Always Easy Being Green)

For the most part, creating a green home isn't all that different from creating a conventional home. An Energy Star–labeled refrigerator, for example, is as good in every way as a refrigerator without the label; what's more, it uses less energy, which saves you money year after year.

But if you've ever spent a day pulling nails out of a heap of salvaged lumber, you'll probably be quick to agree that it isn't always easy being green, especially if it's the reuse aspect of green design that most tickles your fancy. To be frank, heading down the salvaged-materials path usually takes more effort and often costs more money than using conventional new materials.

Depending on your needs and inclinations, greening your home with salvage might be as easy as visiting the showroom of a recovered-wood supplier and putting down a deposit for antique heart pine planks for your kitchen floor. (Easy if you've got the budget; antique wood flooring can run as much as twice the price of hardwood flooring from new-growth trees.)

On the other hand, greening your home with salvage could be as involved as multiple trips to far-flung junkyards as you hunt down that heap of scrap sheet metal that's waiting to be resurrected as exterior siding for the new addition to your house. (Finding the stuff, by the way, is just the beginning. How will you get it home? Where will you store it until you're ready to use it? Is it contaminated with toxins like lead-based paint? How will you install it or who will install it for you? What will the building inspector say? What will your neighbors think? How will it affect the resale value of your house?)

So, is reusing old stuff worth the trouble? That's an individual call. If you decide that the salvage path doesn't suit your temperament or the particular home-improvement project you're planning, keep in mind that there are myriad other ways to green your home (you'll get plenty of ideas for those, too, as you read this book).

Personally, though, I think reuse *is* worth the effort.

Years ago I helped launch a couple of environmental general stores in San Francisco. In keeping with the theme of the eco-friendly products we planned to sell, from organically grown cotton sheets to handbags made from old tires, we built out the stores using salvage wherever we could: oak and glass office doors from the 1940s, well-worn floor boards, shelves fabricated from rusted iron security grates, a whimsical wall-storage unit made from junked refrigerator doors and school lockers. The result? Stores that were fun to shop in and work in because they were loaded with personality and reflected the spirit of the crew that created them.

© 2005 Undine Pröhl

As I write this book, I'm starting on a kitchen remodel and addition at my own house, an 1890s Victorian. I'm grateful to have design help from the talented Cate Leger, an architect whose work is featured in this book. Of course, my partner, Erik, and I want to walk our talk (he works in the building energy-efficiency field), so we'll do the regular good green stuff: beefed-up insulation, double-pane windows, sustainably harvested framing lumber, paints that don't offgas unhealthy chemicals, and other steps that are becoming more mainstream by the day.

We'll also pay attention to reuse and recycling by looking for ways to reduce construction and demolition waste and by choosing recycled-content products like cellulose insulation made from old newspapers. Beyond those more conventional paths to reuse, we plan to use salvaged materials to add pizzazz to the new kitchen. Reclaimed wood flooring, for sure, and maybe countertops of recycled glass or salvaged slate. On the exterior, who knows — perhaps some kind of salvaged metal for the exterior siding and deck railings.

I'm a writer, not an architect, builder or woodworker, so when I look at discarded street signs or junked airplane flaps or a stack of dusty, scarred floorboards in the dark recesses of a salvage yard, it's sometimes a stretch to envision these materials integrated into my home. Fortunately, I've had the pleasure of checking out scores of homes where reuse and salvage have been elevated to an art form. The tips and insights I've gleaned from homeowners, builders and architects with extensive reuse experience are inspiring me to take bolder steps with my own home.

I hope you'll be as jazzed as I am by the homes and people featured in *Redux*. And if you'd like to share your own salvage or green home projects, please contact me through my Web site, www.goodgreenhomes.com.

Five (Relatively) Easy Pieces

© 2005 Edward Caldwell

In this kitchen, the back-splash tiles and bar top are both recycled glass. See more of this house on page 106.

Are you more of a decide-it-yourselfer than a do-it-yourselfer? Don't despair. You can still include salvaged and recycled materials in your home without going to the lengths of carving up a cargo container. Here are a few straightforward suggestions:

1. *Fly ash in concrete.* For any project involving poured concrete, ask your contractor or concrete supplier about high-volume fly ash concrete. Fly ash, a by-product of coal-burning power plants, replaces a portion of the portland cement in concrete. It may not sound sexy but it does the environment a good turn by helping reduce carbon dioxide emissions to the atmosphere. Read about fly ash on page 134.

2. *Reclaimed wood flooring.* Google on "reclaimed wood floor" or "antique wood floor" (or check the Resources section at the back of this book) and you'll find scores of suppliers of finished flooring perfect for any home, including salvaged cypress, heart pine, oak, chestnut, walnut, hemlock and more. Just remember, antique nail holes are beauty marks, not character flaws.

3. *Conventional materials with recycled content.* There's an abundance of recycled-content building products available, including carpet, drywall, plastic lumber for decking and outdoor furniture, fiberglass and cellulose insulation, rubber roofing tiles, and glass kitchen and bath tiles. Look for the highest post-consumer recycled content you can get — post-consumer refers to recyclable trash that's actually kept out of landfills, like the newspapers and bottles we put out for curbside recycling.

4. *Secondhand or antique furniture.* This one's a giveaway for those of us who love browsing antiques stores or flea markets. If you're in the habit of only buying new furniture, consider vintage the next time you're looking to replace a coffee table or set of dining chairs.

5. *Recycled-glass countertops.* Granite and concrete are both popular options for kitchen and bath counters these days. An inspired alternative is a stone-like material made with polished chips of recycled glass. Counter Production in Berkeley, California, is a pioneer in this area.

Introduction · 15

RENOVATION

From a green point of view, renovation has a lot going for it. Reusing a home rather than building from the ground up means you're not encroaching on wildlands or farmlands. Reuse also takes advantage of existing infrastructure — roads, utility lines, sewer services and the like. And unless you're doing a gut remodel that strips the building to its skeleton, reuse uses a lot less stuff, from lumber and drywall to nails and screws.

But don't confuse a regular renovation with a green renovation. Eco-friendly reuse means renovating not just with an eye to updating interiors or adding rooms, but with an emphasis on slashing energy use, protecting natural resources and providing healthy indoor air quality.

Ratchet Up the Reuse

Reusing an existing building is a good green strategy, but why stop there? Ratchet up the reuse by getting creative with salvaged and recycled materials as you renovate your home. Depending on your tastes,

your reuse of old stuff can be subtle or bold, as you'll see in the four homes featured in this section.

In the chapter "Modernism Redux," bamboo cabinet faces conceal cabinet boxes made of strawboard — similar to particleboard but made from waste straw. Stealth reuse, you might call it.

"No House Is an Island" takes us to a Martha's Vineyard home renovated with wood reclaimed from river bottoms and old beer-brewing tanks. What stands out is fine craftsmanship and gorgeous wood, not any sense that the home is built from salvage.

"Out on a Limb" features a 1970s house renovated with fallen oaks. Some of the tree limbs are left in a natural state instead of being squared off, a spirited reminder that our homes do indeed come from the land.

And in "Spare Parts," a condominium complex that's part rehab and part new construction unabashedly sports junked car parts and street signs, daring us to have a little fun with salvage when greening our homes.

^
The Wilsons extended the rear of the house by fourteen feet without conspicuously changing the original modernist exterior. A five-foot overhang was added at the back for weather protection; it also allows the awning windows to be opened for cross ventilation even when it's raining.

Modernism Redux

Where: Alexandria, Virginia

Owners/Architects:
Kendall P. Wilson, Sally Wilson
Ken Wilson is principal of
Envision Design
Washington, D.C.
202.775.9000
envisionsite.com

General Contractor: Courthouse Remodeling

Photographer: Eric Laignel

Mid-Century Modernism Meets Green Design

The sexy pared-down look of mid-twentieth-century design is back in style, with furniture from the likes of Charles and Ray Eames, Eero Saarinen, Florence Knoll Bassett and Isamu Noguchi claiming a place in the canons of interior design. Modernist homes built from the 1930s through the '60s have also proved their enduring appeal, although not all live up to today's performance expectations. Many, for example, are notorious for outsized heating and cooling bills, especially those houses built with the floor-to-ceiling expanses of glass that once heralded a new kind of informal indoor/outdoor lifestyle.

Poorly executed renovations of mid-century modernist houses are a dime a dozen, as owners struggle with adapting floor plans, solving maintenance problems like drainage from nearly flat roofs, and improving energy performance.

But it is possible to get it right *and* make it green, as Ken and Sally Wilson did with their coolly angular home in Alexandria, Virginia. Here, reclaimed and recycled materials remain behind the scenes rather than

< Rain pouring off the low-slope roof had been eroding soil in front of the house. The Wilsons solved the problem by creating a gravel trench laid with a drainage pipe to catch rainwater and slow its release to the soil. Mexican beach pebbles give the area a polished look.

"New" reclaimed brick clads the extension at the back of the house, matching the original reclaimed brick still in place next to the side door and lower window. New cedar siding covers the old T-111 plywood siding.

The front of the house, with its two-story wall of windows, faces south. In the summer, overhangs and shading from trees keep direct sunlight and heat out, while in late fall and winter the lower-angle sun lets in more light and warmth. >

REUSE RECAP

☐ Renovation of mid-twentieth-century modernist house expands square footage by 36 percent and improves energy efficiency while respecting original design

☐ Cabinet boxes in kitchen, bathrooms and dining room made from strawboard

☐ Renovated exterior is clad with salvaged brick to match original salvaged brick siding

☐ Recycled-content fiberglass insulation

MORE GREEN STRATEGIES

☐ Used bamboo cabinet faces in kitchen, bathrooms and dining room

☐ Increased depth of perimeter walls and ceiling cavity to accommodate thicker insulation

☐ Replaced many single-pane windows with double-pane insulating glazing

☐ Replaced inefficient air conditioner with highly efficient unit

☐ Installed Energy Star appliances

☐ Used zero-VOC interior paint (see page 60 for more about VOCs)

☐ Used copper plumbing pipes instead of PVC (see page 127 for more about PVC)

☐ Added roof overhang at rear to protect house from moisture damage

☐ Installed drainage system to stop soil erosion

taking center stage: cabinet boxes of recycled straw are faced with sleek bamboo, reclaimed brick from old industrial buildings blends seamlessly with the original brick cladding, and thick new layers of recycled-content insulation lie snug behind walls and ceilings.

Back to the Future

In 1981, Ken Wilson was fresh out of school and newly on the job at an architecture firm in Washington, D.C. Hearing about a house-sitting opportunity at a vacant residence that was for sale in nearby Alexandria, he jumped at the chance for a home — albeit temporary — of his own.

Lucky for him but not so for the owner, the house languished on the market for six months, a victim of mortgage interest rates in the 15 to 18 percent stratosphere. As he kept an eye on the house, the young architect grew to appreciate the neighborhood, Hollin Hills, a subdivision just outside of D.C.'s Beltway.

Its 450 or so homes were built by developer Robert Davenport over two decades, from 1949 to 1970. Compared to typical post-war suburban tracts, the 240-acre Hollin Hills was cutting edge: it boasted a park-like setting with meandering streets and wooded lots, no fences or other barriers between properties, and homes oriented to respond to topography instead of rigidly lining up to face the street. Hollin Hills is a "really unusual development, especially for Washington, D.C.," says Wilson. "At the time it was thought to be the development of the future."

< The front façade still has its original single-pane windows (large expanses of uninsulated glass are a downside of many mid-century modernist homes), but roll-down shades help keep warmth in at night.

Cabinet boxes in the kitchen and bathroom, as well as the dining room credenza, are PrimeBoard ➤
(primeboard.com), an industrial-grade particleboard made with recycled straw instead of tree fibers
(read more about similar products on page 137). Cabinet faces are bamboo, a fast-growing grass that
can be harvested every three to five years. "We really love the look of it," Ken Wilson says, "and that it's
a more rapidly renewable material" than wood. The renovated kitchen includes an efficient Energy Star
dishwasher and refrigerator, and a built-in center for compost, trash and recyclables in the island.

Inside Scoop

First Stop for Eco-Friendly Renovation: Energy Efficiency

In the long run, the energy your home uses year in and year out has a greater environmental impact than the materials that went into building the home. If you're embarking on a green renovation, energy efficiency should be a top priority, as it was for the Wilsons when they expanded their Virginia home. Energy-efficiency upgrades will lower your utility bills, make your home more comfortable, and help reduce global warming and air pollution.

If you're opening up wall and ceiling cavities, don't miss the opportunity to beef up insulation and seal holes and cracks that allow moisture and air to penetrate. If you plan to replace windows, buy ones appropriate for your climate (the Efficient Windows Collaborative has a great Web site for helping homeowners understand window technology: efficientwindows.org). And seek out energy-efficient heating and cooling equipment and appliances; the Energy Star Web site allows you to compare the energy consumption of hundreds of models of refrigerators, dishwashers, clothes washers, ceiling fans, air conditioners, furnaces and more (energystar.gov).

The original homes, most of which were designed by architect Charles Goodman, were moderately priced but rigorously modern, with large expanses of glass, light-filled interiors, and little superfluous trim or adornment. From the start, Hollin Hills attracted aficionados of modernist architecture as well as artists, academics and others looking for a sub-urban dwelling that didn't conform to the prevailing neocolonial mold.

Wilson recalls that during those months as a Hollin Hills resident, "I really got to see the neighborhood. I always said, 'One day I'm going to make it and come back here.' You know, it's hard to imagine ever being able to afford a house as a young architect."

Green Remodeling, without the Remuddling

Fast forward to 1999, when Wilson, now an established architect with his own Washington-based firm, Envision Design, and his wife, Sally, also an architect (she now works for a major commercial real estate firm), are in the market for a house for themselves and their sons, Isaac and Nathan.

Not surprisingly, they found their way back to Hollin Hills. "It's an incredible place. It's such a great secret," Sally Wilson says. "We looked for a couple of years before we found this house." Her husband adds, "It was on the last street to be developed in the neighborhood. Our house was one of the newest. It was built in 1970, but you can see houses that are very similar designed by Goodman that were built as early as 1949."

The house was essentially a square, rather severe in its simplicity, with

Bamboo cabinets work beautifully with the clean lines of mid-century modernism.

a two-story façade of glass in front and floor-to-ceiling windows in back. "We fell in love with the house," Ken Wilson admits. Three decades hadn't dulled the home's modern edge, but some aspects of its design didn't live up to today's standards. The kitchen was small, not the kind of central gathering place preferred today. Other rooms were also cramped, and the glass walls and flat roof translated to limited closet space and no attic storage.

"We decided to do an addition," Ken Wilson explains, "but we wanted to do it in an incredibly sensitive way. We wanted people to drive by the house and never know there was an addition there, and just think of the house as if it was always intended to be this way."

Pulling out the rear of the house by fourteen feet enabled the Wilsons to expand the kitchen, master bedroom, bathrooms and closets, and to add exercise and storage space and a wine closet in the basement. In total, they beefed up the two-story, 2,800-square-foot house by another 1,000 square feet without distorting the linearity and simplicity of the original design.

"Certainly if we were to build a house from scratch we would have been more aggressive in the environmental side of things," Ken Wilson says. "But what we wanted to do was build an addition that was very sympathetic to the mid-century modern design, and incorporate as much green or smart thinking as possible."

Modernizing Modernism

As part of that smart thinking, the couple put energy efficiency high on their list. One strategy was to find "clever ways that we could make the roof rafters go from the original two-by-eights to two-by-twelves so we could stick a lot more insulation up there but not have it affect the trim lines on the outside of the house," says Ken Wilson. "Also, we thickened the perimeter walls. They're two-by-sixes instead of two-by-fours, to have more insulation." They used fiberglass insulation with 25 percent recycled content and no added formaldehyde (formaldehyde, a respiratory irritant and carcinogen, is a common additive to many building materials including some fiberglass insulation and pressed-wood products).

Although the house badly needed the energy-efficiency upgrade, it did start out with important green design features in its favor, including good solar orientation and shading, and terrific connections with the outdoors. "It's like going to a weekend house every single day," Sally Wilson says.

The front of the house, with its two-story wall of floor-to-ceiling glass, faces predominantly south. Trees and overhangs shade the windows from direct sun in the summertime, while allowing in plenty of light. "It was well designed for daylighting," Ken Wilson says. "We really don't have to turn on any lights until nighttime. Even the bathroom upstairs has a skylight."

In the expanded master bathroom, high windows splash the room with daylight while providing privacy.

New awning windows at ceiling level promote cross ventilation throughout the house, reducing the need for air-conditioning.

The Wilsons swapped out a number of the existing single-glazed windows with insulating double-pane glass, which not only reduces heating and cooling costs but also makes the home more comfortable. They replaced the old gas furnace with a high-efficiency model, and replaced the old 6-SEER air conditioner upstairs (SEER, or Seasonal Energy Efficiency Ratio, indicates an air conditioner's energy efficiency) with a highly efficient 18-SEER unit that has a variable-frequency fan drive. Downstairs, they do without air-conditioning. Thanks to these energy-efficiency upgrades, the Wilsons now use about 13 percent less gas and no additional electricity even though they increased their home's size by 36 percent.

Outside, brick clads the non-glass portions of the first story. In the course of their remodel the Wilsons learned from one of their carpenters, whose father had helped build the Hollin Hills development, that their home's original brick came from demolished industrial buildings in Baltimore. In keeping with the theme of both an aesthetically and environmentally sensitive remodel, additional salvaged brick was found that matched the older material. "The mason did a great job," Ken Wilson says. "It's very hard to tell where the old stops and the new begins."

The same could be said for the renovation as a whole. It's a classic example of how green thinking can be blended with modern design to create a home that will remain up to date for decades to come. ❖

Side Effects

Building Reuse Hierarchy

People often assume that the greenest of homes have to be built from the ground up. But there's good news for those of us who will never get around to building our own abode. Reusing an existing home, whether it's a 30-year-old suburban ranch or a 150-year-old carriage house, is usually much easier on the planet than building new. Of the five building-reuse options listed here, routine maintenance (#1) is the most eco-friendly because it uses the fewest resources and preserves the building for the future. Deconstruction (#5) should be your reuse path of last resort, if none of the other options will do.

1. *Repair and maintain.* Help ensure that the building will remain livable for decades or even centuries by attending to routine maintenance. Moisture damage is the main reason buildings fail, so pay particular attention to gutter blockages, plumbing leaks, rain infiltration and signs of mold. Look for ways to improve drainage of water away from your house, like the Wilsons did with their flat-roofed modernist home in Virginia (page 18). Also look for ways to improve energy efficiency, because your home's biggest drain on the planet's resources comes from the amount of energy it consumes year after year.

2. *Redecorate.* A full-scale remodel can be a resource-intensive process, with mountains of old drywall, lumber, cabinets and appliances coming out, and heaps of new goods coming in. Before plunging into a remodeling project, consider whether redecorating will meet your needs instead. Light-colored paint on walls and ceilings will brighten a space, making it feel larger. Getting rid of clutter can also give you more space. Sinks and cabinet doors can be refinished without scrapping the whole room.

3. *Reduce, reuse and recycle when you remodel.* Construction and demolition debris makes up anywhere from 12 to 30 percent of all waste that ends up in U.S. landfills. But with some advance planning and a focus on the three Rs (reduce, reuse, recycle), you can keep valuable resources out of the landfill. First, look for ways to reduce waste. For example, refinish instead of replacing hardwood floors, sinks and cabinet doors. Second, find ways to reuse the stuff you're pulling out. Reuse framing lumber that's in good shape, move old kitchen cabinets to the garage for extra storage, and so on. What you can't reuse yourself, sell or donate. Finally, recycle what can't be reused: metal and clean wood are often recyclable, whereas painted drywall and materials contaminated with lead-based paint aren't; check with your garbage hauler or municipal recycling program to find out what's recyclable in your area.

4. *Relocate the building.* Do you have a house you can't abide on a piece of property you adore? Rather than demolishing the house so you can start from a clean slate, consider finding a buyer who will move it to another lot. It's no easy feat to move a building lock, stock and barrel, but there are companies that specialize in raising houses off their foundations and transporting them to another site. Look under House Movers in the Yellow Pages or check the International Association of Structural Movers' member listings at iasm.org.

5. *Deconstruct and reuse.* If you need to get rid of a structure and it can't be relocated, check into having it deconstructed — manually dismantled so that its components can be salvaged for other projects. LOCUS Architecture took apart a small house in Minneapolis and used the old lumber and other materials to build a new house; see page 118. Read more about deconstruction on page 126.

Back Story

Green at Home, Green at Work, Green at the Spa

Ken Wilson founded the Washington, D.C.–based Envision Design in 1999. It's a full-service architecture and interior design firm focusing on the sustainable design of commercial office interiors, retail spaces, residential and base building work, and product and exhibit design. Among Envision's clients is a Who's Who list of leading environmental groups, including Greenpeace USA, Environmental Defense, Audubon, Conservation International and World Wildlife Fund.

"With the commercial design work our firm does we try to show that you don't have to give anything up with sustainable design," Wilson says. "You can have a really cool, hip interior space for an office that can be very low impact on the environment, very healthy for the people that work there, and be really cutting-edge design all at the same time. There's no reason you have to give that up."

Envision Design recently completed the design of Nusta Spa, a downtown-Washington day spa (nustaspa.com). Located on the ground floor of an office building, the space underwent radical transformation by Envision Design and general contractor James G. Davis Construction. The team went to great lengths to keep construction and demolition waste to a minimum. Office equipment, furniture and other materials left behind by previous tenants were donated to local nonprofits. Construction and demolition debris was sorted, reused and recycled, with about half of it diverted from disposal in landfills.

Green design features include maple floors from FSC-certified sustainably managed forests (see page 48 for more about the Forest Stewardship Council), FSC-certified plywood underlayment for the hardwood floors, strawboard as the core material for the millwork (see page 137), recycled-content carpet, zero-VOC interior paints, sealants and adhesives (see page 60 for more about VOCs), ceiling tiles salvaged from another project, energy-efficient fluorescent and LED lighting, and an elegant highlight wall milled from reclaimed oak beams.

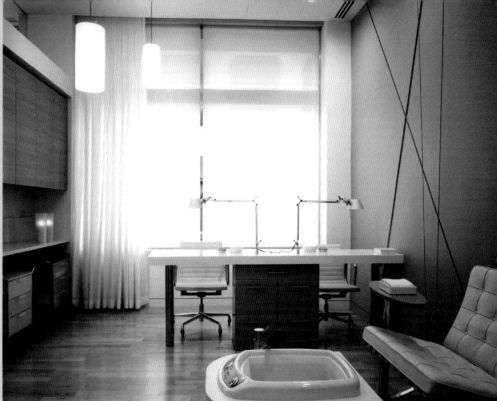

© 2005 Eric Laignel

"Clients love it," says Elizabeth Snowdon, Nusta Spa's president. "They say, 'This is a beautiful space *and* it's green.'" She adds that "the sustainable design piece is absolutely responsible" for the phenomenal name recognition and media attention the spa achieved within its first six months of opening.

Nusta Spa has received Gold Certification under the U.S. Green Building Council's LEED Rating System for Commercial Interiors.*

∧
< Nusta, a day spa in downtown Washington, was designed with reclaimed, recycled and sustainably harvested materials, including FSC-certified maple floors and a wall in the reception area milled from salvaged oak beams.

* The LEED (Leadership in Energy and Environmental Design) Green Building Rating System is a voluntary standard that defines high-performance green buildings. Translation: buildings that are healthier to spend time in, easier on the environment, and more profitable for building owners and tenants. Developed by the nonprofit U.S. Green Building Council, LEED addresses specific markets within the construction industry, including new construction and renovation of commercial buildings, and commercial-building interiors. LEED for Homes was under development as I was writing this book. Find out more: usgbc.org.

© 2005 Randi Baird

No House Is an Island

Where: Martha's Vineyard,
Massachusetts

Designer/Builder:
South Mountain Company
West Tisbury, Massachusetts
somoco.com

Photographers:
Randi Baird, Brian Vanden Brink

Craftsmanship, Community and Environmental Stewardship

The house had gone so far downhill that its owners assumed it wasn't worth
saving. Originally built in 1910 as a summer camp on Martha's Vineyard, the
two-story Tudor-style house was stunningly situated on a rise overlooking
Vineyard Sound and the Elizabeth Islands. But it was in such rough shape that
in the mid-1990s the owners approached South Mountain Company, a design/
build firm on the island, about tearing it down and building a new house.

John Abrams, who founded South Mountain Company in 1975 (it's been a
worker-owned cooperative since 1987), suggested that the owners at least
entertain the possibility of renovating the house rather than knocking it
down. "We actually didn't think we would end up saving it," Abrams says.
"But as we got into it more and more with them, it seemed like a barely
sensible idea. And you know what?" he asks, a shade of impishness in his
voice. "It turned out to be a barely sensible idea — but it *was* sensible."

< For the new siding and roofing, South Mountain
Company used white cedar shingles from Maibec,
a Canadian company that buys a large percentage
of its cedar logs from an FSC-certified forestry
company in Maine.

© 2005 Brian Vanden Brink

In the dining room, an addition to the original house, exposed timbers are salvaged Douglas fir from a mill building in Maine built in the early 1900s. The light fixture was designed and built by South Mountain Company.

The trestle table is old-growth "sinker" cypress from the bottom of ❯ the Choctawhatchee River in Florida's panhandle. Back when floating logs downriver was a cheap way to get them to sawmills, loggers didn't worry if a few so-called "deadheads" or "sinkers" sunk to the bottom because first-growth forests seemed limitless. These days, salvagers go to great lengths to recover these high-quality logs. SMC buys them from a salvager in northwestern Florida, who mills them into rough boards. The boards are then shipped to a kiln in Massachusetts, where they are dried and dressed to SMC's specifications.

Abrams recalls that during the renovation, "We saved all the interior doors, which had a lovely pattern. They had six or eight coats of paint on them. When we took off all the paint, underneath was cypress. That's kind of rare around here, but it is our bread-and-butter wood — we use a tremendous amount of salvage cypress that comes off river bottoms in the South. It was a great match."

REUSE RECAP

- ❑ Project was reconceived as renovation rather than tear-down
- ❑ Exterior detailing and deck railings are cypress from dismantled beer tanks
- ❑ Exterior trim, screen doors and dining table are cypress from "sinker" logs recovered from river bottoms
- ❑ Decking is salvaged Douglas fir from racks that once supported whiskey barrels in a Canadian distillery
- ❑ Exposed timbers in dining room are salvaged Douglas fir from an early 1900s mill building in Maine
- ❑ Front door and screen door are from a Nebraska brewery's redwood beer tanks
- ❑ Wood floors and stairs are Southern longleaf pine salvaged from industrial buildings in New England
- ❑ Slate floors, counters and backsplashes are reclaimed roof tiles

MORE GREEN FEATURES

- ❑ Most wood not from salvaged sources is FSC-certified or locally harvested
- ❑ New foundation built to ensure house will last for generations (old house was on rock piers sitting on sand)
- ❑ Emphasis on quality construction and creating a house that will age well
- ❑ Owners provided with an "Owner's Manual" describing sources of salvaged materials, and operating and maintenance instructions for the house

^ Wood floors and stairs are Southern longleaf pine from heavy
timbers salvaged from industrial buildings in New England.

A Good Save

The 5,500-square-foot house was plenty big but had flaws ranging from serious structural failings to outdated room layouts. The second floor was a warren of tiny dark bedrooms that failed to capitalize on the property's dramatic views. And although it was not the owners' primary residence, it needed to be upgraded for year-round use. "From the beginning we were exploring with the owners what they really wanted in a house," Abrams remembers, "and it turned out that they could get what they wanted in a house in *that* house, with very little addition and just by reconfiguring the spaces. It turned out that the space lent itself to satisfying their needs."

"One of the things we had to do to save the house and make it a year-round house was put a foundation under it," Abrams recalls. "There was no foundation. It was just sitting on rock piers on the sand. The usual methods of jacking up and supporting a house and digging a foundation underneath would have destroyed the place completely. So we took the floors out and we vacuumed the sand out. That's how we dug the foundation — with a vacuum cleaner. It worked like a charm."

The front door and screen door are made from redwood salvaged from beer tanks at the Falstaff Brewery in Lincoln, Nebraska, when the company switched to steel tanks.

Much of the house did have to be rebuilt, but the South Mountain team saved and restored important elements, including posts and beams, ceiling joists, fireplaces, all interior doors and some flooring. "The materials and the parts of the house that we saved were uniformly good," Abrams says. "Some things would have been very hard to replace, like the four beach stone fireplaces. Where do you get beach stone?"

Inside Scoop

Tips for Buying Salvaged Wood

Still wondering if reclaimed wood is right for you? Consider these statistics from the environmental advocacy group Natural Resources Defense Council (nrdc.org):

❑ Half the planet's original forests are gone.

❑ Global consumption of wood is expected to increase 50 percent by 2050.

❑ Americans consume 27 percent of all wood commercially harvested worldwide, although the United States represents only 5 percent of the world's population.

By using reclaimed wood, you can help reduce pressure to harvest our remaining old-growth forests. Keep in mind these pointers when looking for salvaged wood:

❑ *Get it from a distributor.* South Mountain Company manages to use so much salvaged wood because they invest heavily in buying it directly from the source and inventorying it in large quantities. You or your general contractor probably won't go to those lengths but that doesn't mean you're out of luck. Rather than buying salvaged materials from the source — whether it's a brewery replacing its redwood tanks or a salvager hauling up logs from a river bottom — buy your materials from lumberyards, salvage yards or other retailers that specialize in reclaimed wood.

I ask Abrams if in the end the renovation truly was worthwhile or if starting with a clean slate might have been a wiser path. "Everybody felt that it was absolutely worth saving, but that was looking back," he says, laughing. "When we were in the middle of it, maybe nobody voiced it, but I'm sure there were a lot of questions, especially on the part of the owners! But there was no question that the result was very satisfying."

Salvaged Lumber Enhances Craftsman Style

The new house retains some of the proportions and design features of the old house — the welcoming front porch, the decorative half-timbering on the façade, deep overhangs over the elongated rear porch, and multiple dormers in the steeply sloping roof. "We often work in our own version of a Craftsman style," Abrams explains. "The simple elements of the original house were particularly well suited to blend with that style. It became very much a Craftsman-style renovation, so the detailing you see is our version of the Arts & Crafts movement."

Over the years, South Mountain Company has earned a reputation for building distinctive homes and furnishings using the finest quality woods. And since the mid-1990s, when they made a commitment to no longer source new wood from old-growth forests, they've continued to maintain their high levels of workmanship while using primarily salvaged lumber. Today more than 90 percent of the exposed interior and exterior woodwork in the homes they build is reclaimed, according to Abrams. Where salvage isn't appropriate, they rely on locally harvested timber and on sustainably harvested wood certified by the FSC.

When I press him to tell me about the salvaged materials in this particular home, Abrams says modestly, "Since all of our projects use a lot of salvage, there was nothing staggering here." But in fact the range of salvaged sources is impressive. Besides reusing materials from the original structure, the renovation included cypress from "sinker" logs dredged from river bottoms; redwood and cypress from beer tanks at two different breweries; Douglas fir from racks that supported a distillery's whiskey barrels and from a dismantled mill building; Southern longleaf pine from industrial buildings in the Northeast; cypress from a brine tank that was spared during a disastrous fire at Malden Mills in Lawrence, Massachusetts; and slate floors, counters and backsplashes from rooftops in Vermont.

When the renovation was complete, SMC provided the owners with an "Owner's Manual," a handbook of operating and maintenance instructions for the house, similar to an owner's manual for a car. The manual also describes the source of all the salvaged materials, so the history of this "new" old house can be treasured for generations. ❖

"Therefore, when we build, let us think that we build forever. Let it not be for present delight, nor for present use alone; let it be such work as our descendants will thank us for, and let us think, as we lay stone on stone, that a time is to come when those stones will be held sacred because our hands have touched them, and that men will say as they look upon the labour and wrought substance of them, 'See! this our fathers did for us.'"

–John Ruskin, *Seven Lamps of Architecture,* 1849

❏ *Get it while you can.* When building with reclaimed wood, keep in mind that quantities are likely to be limited. If you're building a ceiling out of vinegar-barrel staves and you run out partway through the project, you may not be able to find more that are perfect matches. So unless a mismatched look works with your design scheme, buy a sufficient quantity at the outset.

❏ *Get it from a reputable source.* Don't promote the removal of timbers from historically important structures or the salvaging of deadfall from lakes and rivers. (*Deadfall* refers to trees that died naturally and fell into rivers or lakes, where their branches and roots may provide habitat for fish and other organisms. *Sinker logs* or *deadhead,* on the other hand, refer to cut logs that sank as they were being floated downriver to a sawmill. Compared to deadfall, sinkers are believed to have lower value as aquatic habitat because they're stripped clean of branches and roots.) Always purchase salvaged wood from a reputable dealer who knows where the material came from and the conditions under which it was removed. Better yet, look for wood-products operations that have been awarded the Rediscovered Wood certification from SmartWood, a project of the Rainforest Alliance. Find out more at rainforest-alliance.org.

Back Story

Principled Business and Devotion to Craft: John Abrams on South Mountain Company

South Mountain Company was founded in 1975 on Martha's Vineyard by John Abrams and Mitchell Posin. In 1987, the design/build firm restructured as a worker-owned cooperative. SMC now has about thirty workers, sixteen of whom are also owners who share both the profits and the responsibility for company policy. SMC, which designs and builds homes only on Martha's Vineyard, currently has annual sales in the range of $5 to $6 million. Abrams has written a book about business, *The Company We Keep: Reinventing Small Business for People, Community, and Place,* published in 2005. He spoke with me by phone from SMC's 10,000-square-foot facility in West Tisbury, Massachusetts, a few weeks after the company had installed a 100-foot wind turbine that would generate much of their electricity needs.

Q: In the mid-1990s South Mountain Company decided to purchase wood primarily from salvaged sources. What led the owner-employees to that decision?

A: The reason we did it was that we were used to using very, very good woods, and after a time it felt like — all of this old-growth timber — it just felt unconscionable to be using it. So we thought, there's got to be another way.

Q: What were some of the challenges in making the transition to salvaged wood?

A: It was easy to make the commitment. It was hard to do it. We really had to change our operations. And in fact, people didn't like it at first because they were used to working with very fine woods. The salvage woods, it turned out, are even finer, but they take so much preparation and so much mess and entirely different techniques and so much prospecting for metal, that people felt like it was a big bother, it was dirty, it was wasteful because you ended up with so much crap.

And now it's so institutionalized and it brings so much good feeling that nobody can imagine doing it any other way. They're generally uncomfortable if they have to use some fancy new wood.

It *is* hard. It's a huge investment to inventory enough so that you can do what you really need to do. But what makes it easier at this point is that there is quite a little network of suppliers of salvage lumber nationwide. So people don't have to do what we do. They can buy it; they can order it. But it's a lot more fun this way, and it allows us to more competitively use these materials because we source

them directly; we buy them wholesale.

Q: You must have an excellent network of sources at this point. Do you have suppliers coming to you saying, "Look what we just got in?"

A: We do. We hear about things, but we also have a number of suppliers who know what we're looking for, and when they run into it we get a call. So it's really easy to find stuff at this point.

But sometimes the situations are unusual. Sometimes there's an opportunity, you'll get a call — "Pick's Pickles in Toronto is dismantling as we speak 400 tanks, if you get up there in the next few days you might be able to get some." So you hop on a plane, you go up to Pick's Pickles and see the dead birds floating around in the brine, and you go, "Oh my god, this is horrible." But the wood looks great! Sometimes you really have to hop on it. And you have to know what you're looking at.

Q: A few years back, South Mountain Company built a co-housing development on Martha's Vineyard and these days you're also involved with developing affordable housing. What draws you into these community issues?

The South Mountain Company team. The wind turbine in the background, installed ❯ in 2004, produces much of the facility's electricity. Photo © 2005 Bob Gothard.

SMC completed their current facility in West Tisbury, Massachusetts, in 1999. It's one large connected building with about 3,000 square feet of warehouse space for storing lumber, a 4,000-square-foot woodworking shop, and a 3,000-square-foot office and design studio. "It keeps evolving," Abrams says. "We now use biodiesel to heat the building and run our forklifts and trucks." Photo © 2005 Randi Baird.

A: At this point it feels like our purpose is as much making this a great place to live for people that come after us. Our profits are by and large directed to that. When you have a group of people that own the company and live in the community that the company is in, there's a tremendous amount of self-interest in improving the community because this is your community. So that is where a lot of our efforts go.

Q: What would you like South Mountain Company to be known for? What would you like to be known for?

A: For principled business. For good people being devoted to craft and dedicated to building community. And I guess I'd like to be known as the person who began something of lasting value and then became a part of it, a part of making all those good things. The one who had the original vision but whose original vision turned out to be mighty limited. It's something that I began but now I'm much more a part of it rather than "it."

Side Effects

Using Salvage on a Smaller Scale

Interested in giving salvage a try without getting in over your head? There are an infinite number of ways to incorporate small amounts of scrap into your home.

Architect Donna Schumacher often uses salvage to introduce character to homes that may be lacking panache. You don't need to entirely rebuild the structure, even if the house is a "junky box," says Schumacher, of the San Francisco firm X:architecture/Art. "You can use an old door to change the character."

She cautions that some builders will resist using salvage, not just because of added labor but because the material may be less than pristine. While the owner and architect may view the imperfections as marks of character, the builder might well see them as defects that reflect on the quality of his or her work. Schumacher says that it's important to be persistent and persuasive when working with a reluctant contractor, and to have the owner clearly on the side of using salvage.

Schumacher will sometimes accompany clients to salvage yards to pick out doors, windows and other materials. Remodeling with salvage requires a certain frame of mind, she admits, and "it's never less expensive." Even if the door or old lumber costs very little, prepping and installing it can exceed the cost of buying and installing brand-new products, especially in regions of the country where labor rates are high. To make an installation go more smoothly, she will sometimes have salvaged doors framed off-site by a door fabricator so that the builder doesn't have to get bogged down in constructing the frame. For more about Schumacher's work, check out her Web site at xaa.net.

A skylight and large windows animate what was once a dreary laundry room. Photos © 2005 Rebecca Bausher.

A boxy rear addition, formerly a laundry room, was converted into a lively light-filled studio.

French doors picked up at a salvage yard add style to this remodeled bedroom.

^
A 10,000-gallon stainless-steel tank below the deck stores rainwater for irrigation. The deck's and trellis's structural members are old-growth redwood salvaged from a deconstructed sawmill. The home's original deck had badly deteriorated, so it was dismantled, with salvageable boards reused for the new decking.

Out on a Limb

Where: Contra Costa County, California

Architect:
Leger Wanaselja Architecture
Berkeley, California
510.848.8901
lwarc.com

Owners/Builders: Suzanne Jones and Rob Elia

Photographer: Linda Svendsen

A Toppled Oak Sets the Tone for the Renovation of a 1970s Home

"If I had known what I was getting into —" Suzanne Jones breaks off with a laugh. Four years after plunging in, she's close to wrapping up a top-to-bottom renovation of her house in an agricultural area twenty miles east of San Francisco. Jones and her husband, Rob Elia, enlisted green-design firm Leger Wanaselja Architecture to come up with a vision for revamping the thirty-year-old house. But it was Jones, with no previous building experience under her belt, who took on the role of general contractor.

"It was a very challenging experience," she admits. "In fact, I look at it as the hardest thing I've ever done in my life. I wrote a PhD thesis in physics and that was easier than doing this! It took completely different kinds of skills."

< Built in the mid-1970s, the house was renovated to make it more comfortable, energy efficient, and to open up the living spaces to views and light. The great room's three double-hung windows face south, ideal for passive solar heating.

^
Sheltering the entry, an overhang rests on limbs from an old oak that toppled nearby.

The ceiling and beams are original. To update and brighten the home, Jones painted the ceiling beams white (they had been painted dark brown) and had the dark-stained fireplace sand-blasted. Interior spaces were reconfigured and interior walls removed to create a dramatic great room. A small bedroom once occupied the space where the kitchen is now, at right. The columns, bar top and adjacent table, as well as the breakfast nook in the background, are fashioned from two coast live oaks that fell on Jones's and a neighbor's property. >

REUSE RECAP

- ❏ Expanded livable space to 2,400 square feet from 1,900 square feet without increasing footprint
- ❏ Fallen oaks salvaged for interior and exterior posts, counters, furniture, stairs and railing
- ❏ Original redwood trim reused for fencing
- ❏ New exterior siding milled from floor joists from deconstructed military building
- ❏ Underside of entryway roof made from reclaimed tongue-and-groove pine
- ❏ Deteriorated deck rebuilt, with salvageable boards planed and reused
- ❏ Deck's new structural members and trellis built from old-growth redwood rescued from deconstructed sawmill building
- ❏ Maple flooring salvaged from a 1920s post office
- ❏ Master bedroom closet lined with storm-felled cedar from President Andrew Jackson's estate
- ❏ Book shelves, office cabinets, loft ladder and other millwork from reclaimed wood sourced from salvage yards and rundown structures on owner's and brother's properties

MORE GREEN FEATURES

- ❏ Three-kilowatt solar-electric system
- ❏ Rooftop solar collectors for water heating
- ❏ Energy-efficiency upgrades included replacing single-pane windows with double-pane, low-e windows; insulating walls with recycled cellulose and ceiling with polyisocyanurate foam; and installing a light-colored metal roof that reflects heat
- ❏ No air-conditioning; passive solar design moderates indoor temperatures; distributed thermal mass provided by masonry fireplace, thicker than aver-age drywall (5/8 inch) with plaster veneer, and slate floors
- ❏ Kitchen cabinet doors are bamboo; cabinet boxes are FSC-certified maple
- ❏ 10,000-gallon stainless-steel tank stores rainwater for irrigation
- ❏ Dual-flush toilets reduce water use

Making the House – and the World – a Little Bit Better

Jones acknowledges that "the environmental part was what stimulated me to take on this project. I used to be a physicist and then I worked in disarmament and arms control for a number of years, and then got interested in global energy supply and renewable energy. That's what started it," she adds with a laugh, "writing papers about renewable energy and sustainability, but not having actually done anything concrete to advance those objectives. I really wanted to be able to have something where I could say, 'I did this. I did my little part to make the world a little bit better.'"

Renovation didn't figure into Jones's and Elia's original plans, however. "We were thinking we would try to buy a lot and build a strawbale house," Jones says. "Then we found this house, and I thought it's actually nicer in a way to take a house that's not energy efficient and not green and make it into something that is, as opposed to building something new."

Perched at the end of a steep gravel drive, the house had 1,900 square feet of living space on the main floor. The lower level offered potential for more room, with nearly 500 square feet of unfinished space that backs into the slope on the home's north side.

Built in the mid-1970s, the house had good southern exposure, lovely views of a pasture and oak-studded hills, and attractive design features including high ceilings, exposed beams and a massive stone fireplace. The home had worked well for the retired couple who built it thirty years ago, but for a younger couple with plans to start a family, changes to the

< The contemporary style of the new kitchen sets off the organic forms of the oak columns and slabs. The tree limbs reach up to the ceiling beams like branches stretching toward the sun. Cabinets and the work island are faced with bamboo. The bar can be rolled out to the deck when the couple entertains, and the adjacent table can be picked up and moved to serve as an extra dining table. Scott McGlashan, working with Leger Wanaselja Architecture, designed and built the breakfast nook, bar and table.

Inside Scoop

Wood Woes

❏ *Bugs and salvaged wood.* Bugs eat trees. That's why some suppliers of reclaimed flooring and lumber sell only kiln-dried wood; the kiln's heat wipes out those pesky critters. If you're buying salvaged lumber and are worried about bugs, ask if it has been kiln-dried. If you're milling your own lumber from trees that fell on your property, you may have to contend with insects even if you thoroughly air-dry the wood after milling it. One option is to treat the wood with boric acid, which is derived from borax, a low-toxic mineral. Boric acid can be mixed with water and sprayed on the wood, but repeated applications may be necessary, and it isn't always 100 percent effective at eliminating every bug. Another option is to check with small local sawmills to see if you can gain access to a kiln. I've also heard of people running slabs of wood through a carbon dioxide chamber at an art museum (it's used to eradicate bugs from fragile frames and other wooden objects). But don't count on having that option available to you, and don't say I didn't warn you — isn't always easy being green.

❏ *Reclaimed wood and building codes.* Building codes and practices vary from state to state and city to city. In some regions it may be difficult to get building officials to approve the use of reclaimed wood for structural purposes (new lumber is inspected and graded for strength and quality by a certified grader; reclaimed lumber rarely is). Ask for advice from structural engineers in your area, or limit your use of reclaimed wood to nonstructural applications. For new structural lumber that's eco-friendly, buy wood certified by the FSC to have been sustainably harvested.*

* The Forest Stewardship Council is an international certification organization that has established voluntary forest-management standards. FSC-labeled wood products give consumers assurance that the wood comes from sustainably managed forests, so old-growth trees, biodiversity and water quality are protected, and the needs of local people who depend on the forest are respected. FSC-certified wood is increasingly available and cost competitive. Learn more at fsc.org. For a directory of FSC-certified lumber or products, go to certifiedwood.org.

> *"What kind of world do we intend, and how might we design things in keeping with that vision?"*
>
> —William McDonough and Michael Braungart, *Cradle to Cradle*

compartmentalized interior were in order. Architects Karl Wanaselja and Cate Leger worked out a scheme to reconfigure the floor plan to improve flow between rooms and open up living spaces to light and views, without expanding the home's footprint.

An energy-efficiency overhaul was also a top priority; inadequate insulation meant that on winter nights, even with the heat cranked up, Jones and Elia could see their breath as they ate dinner. The house was structurally sound, but the roof, exterior siding, trim and decking had deteriorated and needed replacement. Jones hired carpenter Wayne Pickrell to do much of the major work including framing, roofing, siding and windows.

A Tree Falls, and a Renovation Takes Shape

Wanaselja and Leger have a penchant for using salvaged materials in new contexts, and in Suzanne Jones and Rob Elia they found like-minded clients.

I meet Jones for the first time on a cloudless September morning that promises to be a scorcher. Eight months pregnant with her first child (baby Dean was born in October), she's slightly breathless as she shows me around the almost-completed house.

Homeowner Rob Elia, a fan of mid-century modern design, has used the Internet to track down many used, mint-condition pieces. These classic Eames chairs look right at home in his 1970s house updated for the twenty-first century. The maple floor was salvaged from a 1920s post office in Los Angeles.

Standing outside the front door, I run my hand along the post that supports the roof over the entryway. No ordinary squared-off timber, this is a hefty limb of an old oak, hand-stripped of its bark and sanded to a smooth sheen.

Jones explains that shortly after she and her husband embarked on the renovation, a grand oak toppled near the house. "It was probably a hundred-year-old tree," she says. "We were pretty sad. I could see it through my kitchen window. We stared at it for a long time. There was one branch in particular that looked like it would be perfect for the king post inside. I wasn't quite sure if we could make it work, but Karl came out and looked at it and thought we could. Actually it was a nice way to get a positive out of a negative."

They wound up salvaging that tree as well as another old oak that fell on their neighbor's property. Some of the larger limbs were used for structural posts inside and to support the entry roof outside. Jones readily acknowledges how much effort it took to transform the limbs into usable posts that still retain the tree's essential form. Fred Hyer of Leger Wanaselja Architecture worked with Jones to chisel off the thickest bark by hand. They removed the remaining bark with a grinding disc and then used a random orbital sander to get the wood smooth. Limbs destined for the interior posts got a final hand-sanding and were treated with a linseed oil–based finish. Exterior posts were weatherproofed with polyurethane. It's the kind of labor-intensive project that many general contractors would hesitate to take on, but for Jones, as an owner-builder, it was a labor of love. She's quick, however, to give

Hyer main credit for designing, finishing and installing the posts.

Jones also salvaged the oaks' trunks. She had them milled into slabs ranging from one-and-a-half to two-and-a-half inches thick, and air-dried the slabs for two years, treating them repeatedly with a boric acid solution to get rid of bugs. Eventually the trunk slabs were fashioned into tops for the kitchen island as well as the table and bar that separate the kitchen from the dining area. The oak trees, Jones notes, have never left the site. They grew for a hundred years or more on this land, and then after they died naturally, they were milled in her driveway, dried in her garage and now grace her home.

Jones speculates that if ten years earlier she had dreamed about the kind of house she would be living in today, "I don't think I would have ever pictured anything like this. I'm really pleased that it turned out to be something different and interesting. I didn't really know anything about green design or contemporary design or modern furniture. All these people have come into my life, my husband, and Cate and Karl and everybody, and it's led to something that's unexpected but really appreciated." ❖

Salvaging the oaks was a labor of love that paid off handsomely.

‹ Sarah Hoffmann, who raises sheep for cheese production in Weston, Missouri, built a lambing barn with mostly salvaged goods, including stained-glass windows found on eBay. The structural wood is Southern longleaf pine reclaimed from a local hundred-year-old warehouse. Other materials bought from salvage yards and online include gates, doors, wood paneling and trim, a sink, and an old choir rail from a dismantled church used as a railing in the barn's loft. Photo © 2005 Sarah Hoffman.

Side Effects

Where to Find Good Old Stuff

Flummoxed about where to find vinegar-barrel staves for your cathedral ceiling or weathered slate roofing tiles for your kitchen floors?

There's no shortage of outlets for antiques, vintage furniture and plain old junk: yard sales, flea markets, thrift stores, antiques shops, auctions — you've likely been there and done that. But if you're in the market for used materials to build with, not just to decorate with, you may need to look further afield. Here are ideas gleaned from my forays into salvage seeking, as well as interviews with connoisseurs of building salvage and other good junk.

❏ *Salvage yards and building-material reuse stores.* Salvage yards carry an astounding array of treasures and tripe, from sleek granite counters to cheesy particleboard cabinets. Not everything at salvage yards is salvaged; some yards also carry manufacturer's seconds, overruns and other good-as-new products. Suzanne Jones, whose home is featured in this chapter, lucked upon a brand-name, brand-new jetted tub at Urban Ore, a popular salvage yard in Berkeley, California. Covered in dust but otherwise pristine, it happened to be the exact size she needed. She paid a fraction of what it would have cost at a regular retail store.

For salvage yards near you, check the Yellow Pages under Salvage Merchandise; Building Materials—Architectural, Antique & Used; Lumber—Used; and Junk Dealers. Habitat for Humanity, the national nonprofit builder of affordable housing, runs many Habitat ReStores that sell used and surplus building materials; get info at habitat.org/env/restores.aspx.

❏ *Reclaimed wood specialists.* Twenty years ago, if you lusted after an antique heart pine floor, you might have had to dismantle a derelict warehouse and mill the wood yourself. Thankfully for those of us

not inclined to erect a mini-sawmill in our garages, more and more companies specialize in selling finished flooring, furniture and other products made from reclaimed wood. EcoTimber sells reclaimed wood flooring, as well as wood flooring certified to have come from sustainably managed forests, and wood alternatives like bamboo. They're in San Rafael, California, but they market their products nationally (ecotimber.com). The Woods Company of Chambersburg, Pennsylvania, sells finished flooring from lumber salvaged from aged barns, rural buildings, factories and warehouses (thewoodscompany.com). Whit McLeod makes classic Craftsman furniture from salvaged materials. I own a couple of his folding deck chairs fashioned from the grape-stained staves of wine barrels (whitmcleod.com).

❏ *Online resources.* Many Web sites specialize in matching up people who want to get rid of junk with people looking for vintage treasures ("buy junk, sell antique," as the saying goes). Merchandise skews more toward furniture than building materials, but pretty much everything can be had online these days. In some ways, the Internet has simplified the hunt for old stuff, although competition may be stiffer because unlike bricks-and-mortar stores, the Web cuts across geographic boundaries. The best known of the Internet auction sites is probably eBay.com. Craigslist.org is a giant community bulletin board where you can sell, give away, buy or barter used goods. Freecycle.org is an online network with the mission of "helping to foster a local gifting community." Everything on the Freecycle Network is given away for free, from pianos to fax machines to old doors.

❏ *Scrap dealers.* There's a thriving market here and overseas for recyclable scrap metal so most of it gets sorted, crushed and shipped out before you can say, "Hold that I-beam." But if you're looking for something specific, introduce yourself to the scrap dealers in your region (look in the Yellow Pages or online under Scrap Metals). Finding the perfect piece of scrap metal is a tricky mix of persistence, good relationships and serendipity. Karl Wanaselja, an architect and builder, haunts local junkyards. A scrap metal dealer who knew Wanaselja gave him a call when a heap of old street and highway signs landed in his yard. See the results on page 54.

❏ *Architectural salvage stores.* These shops don't always carry bread-and-butter building materials like lumber or flooring, but they can't be beat for cool design details and unique furnishings, from nineteenth-century marble mantels to stained-glass windows to period light fixtures. My father has whiled away many an hour at United House Wrecking's emporium in Stamford, Connecticut (unitedhousewrecking.com). They carry a mind-boggling array of both vintage items and reproductions. For similar stores near you, look in the Yellow Pages or online under Architectural Salvage.

❏ *Building deconstruction sales.* Deconstruction companies take apart buildings board by board and sell what's salvageable, usually through an affiliated salvage yard (for more about deconstruction, see page 126). Some companies hold pre-deconstruction sales at the site of the building that's coming down; you show up at the property on a designated day and make an offer on whatever catches your fancy. A few years back I checked out a deconstruction sale at a grand old school for girls in San Jose, California. I didn't bring home any treasures — the institutional scale of the building's components would have dwarfed my little Victorian house — but I gawked as colossal chandeliers, staircases, mantels, tile work and other prizes got snapped up.

❏ *Dumpster diving.* It's amazing what people throw away. Carl Scheidenhelm, an architect in San Francisco, once came upon a pair of tall Herculite doors — full-glass frameless panels — in a Dumpster in San Francisco's financial district. The doors, which he guesses are from the 1940s, now grace the back of his house, opening onto a deck and garden. I confess that I can rarely walk by a Dumpster without taking a peek inside.

The building on the left, which dates to the early twentieth century, was originally a market with two apartments above. Leger Wanaselja Architecture transformed it into three homes and a commercial unit. The building on the right is new construction, with four condos and a street-level commercial unit.

Spare Parts

Where: Berkeley, California

Developer, architect and builder: Leger Wanaselja Architecture
510.848.8901
lwarc.com

Photographers: Cesar Rubio Photography, Karl Wanaselja

‹ Unique materials are one antidote to increasing conformity and standardization in our buildings and our lives. Note the street-sign gate; railings made of bent signs; Mazda and Porsche hatchback awnings over doors; and highway signs cladding the roof decks, bay and underside of the stairs.

Condos Clad in Road Signs Revive a Neglected Property

Pause at the hectic intersection of Dwight Way and M. L. King Jr. Way in Berkeley, California, and chances are you'll notice a thing or two out of the ordinary about the condo complex on the corner. For one, there's the pedestrian gate between the complex's two buildings — a slightly madcap picket fence made of green-and-white street signs. Rainbow Ridge Road. Blue Horizon Drive. Epic Avenue. "Do such places really exist?" you might wonder as your car idles at the light.

Another day your gaze might linger on a curved glass awning above a door-way. After a double-take or two, it may dawn on you that you're looking at a window removed from a car's hatchback. It's so attuned to its new function that it's as if the automobile designer had anticipated how the window might someday be reincarnated.

At dusk you might admire the silvery sheen of the metal cladding on the buildings' bays. True, the siding's a bit unusual: large rectangles of smooth aluminum, not the corrugated metal sheets often used in contemporary

© 2005 Cesar Rubio

Between the buildings, a gate made of salvaged retroreflective street signs marks the pedestrian entrance.

Small but airy, the homes were built with healthy materials, including plaster veneer on walls, zero-VOC paint on walls that aren't plastered, and natural oil finishes on wood trim and doors. >

REUSE RECAP

- ❏ Rehab of run-down building and neglected urban property
- ❏ Reuse of junked street signs and car parts
- ❏ Reuse of nearly all framing lumber, flooring, trim, doors and door jambs
- ❏ Extensive use of wood salvaged from buildings and storm-felled trees
- ❏ Recycled content in kitchen counters, insulation and concrete
- ❏ Careful management of construction waste including sale or donation of usable materials, composting of clean wood scraps and recycling of all metal

MORE GREEN FEATURES

- ❏ Design emphasizes energy efficiency, passive solar heating and daylighting
- ❏ Photovoltaic panels create electricity from sunlight (installed on one unit)
- ❏ Energy Star appliances are used
- ❏ All new two-by-six framing lumber is FSC certified; two-by-six studs (instead of standard two-by-fours) allow for extra-thick insulation at exterior walls
- ❏ Low- or zero-VOC interior paints are used
- ❏ Plaster on most interior walls reduces need for paint, caulk and trim
- ❏ Interior woodwork is finished with natural oils
- ❏ Cabinet boxes are made of medium-density fiberboard with no added formaldehyde
- ❏ In parking area, permeable decomposed granite paving and drywells keep storm-water runoff on-site, replenishing groundwater instead of draining to municipal sewer system
- ❏ Native and drought-resistant landscaping

© 2005 Karl Wanaselja

^ A colorful detail of the concrete floor in one of the units. The developers used approximately 100 yards of concrete with 50 percent recycled fly ash content. For more about fly ash, see page 134.

© 2005 Cesar Rubio

^ Cool junk may be what attracts attention outside, but the overall design is rooted in smart building science. The homes are energy efficient, with higher levels of cellulose insulation sprayed into wall and ceiling cavities than required by code, and Energy Star appliances (energystar.gov). Kitchen counters are recycled glass from Counter Production (counterproduction.com).

> *"The profligate habits of our own country and our own time — the sheer volume of the garbage that we create and must dispose of — will make our society an open book. The question is: Would we ourselves recognize our story when it is told, or will our garbage tell tales about us that we as yet do not suspect?"*
>
> –William Rathje and Cullen Murphy, *Rubbish! The Archaeology of Garbage*

design. It's not until you look underneath one of the bays, where the siding is flipped right side out, that you get it. These are highway signs, with black letters on a vivid orange background warning of detours, construction zones and other hazards of the open road.

What's going on here?

Karl Wanaselja and Cate Leger are at it again. As architects, builders and developers, their firm Leger Wanaselja Architecture has earned a reputation for creating homes that marry the basic tenets of green building — healthy materials and efficient use of energy and resources — to a high-spirited style that celebrates the aesthetic and functional qualities of good old-fashioned junk.

Protecting Greenbelts by Building in Town

Their condo complex, with a total of nine units, hits just about every green building target you can name. It's a mixed-use infill project, combining commercial and residential spaces on an underutilized urban lot. Mixed use and infill developments help make cities vibrant places and reduce pressure to sprawl into outlying farmland and open space. "We're five blocks from BART," the Bay Area's rapid transit system, Wanaselja points out. "We're walkable to downtown and campus, bikeable everywhere in Berkeley. No new services have to be provided through any pristine wildlands."

Inside Scoop

The Air You Breathe

Ever notice that new-paint smell in a building? If so, you're breathing volatile organic compounds, or VOCs, that are offgassing from fresh paint. VOCs, a class of organic chemicals that readily evaporate at room temperature, occur naturally in many materials. They are also added to an array of building products, including many types of particleboard, paint, solvents, carpets and fabrics.

Exposure to VOCs can cause symptoms ranging from nausea, eye irritation and head-aches to more severe, longer-lasting effects. The VOCs in paint and other products also contribute to the formation of smog outside.

For healthier indoor air quality, use solvent-free adhesives, and water-based, low- or no-VOC interior paints and sealants. Green Seal, a nonprofit group that sets voluntary environmental and health standards for prod-ucts, recommends using interior paints that don't exceed 50 grams per liter of VOCs for flat paint or 150 grams per liter for non-flat paint (greenseal.org). You'll find the VOC levels listed on the paint can's label. Most major paint companies offer at least one very low-VOC product, and some companies, like AFM Safecoat, offer a full line of zero-VOC paints and sealants (afmsafecoat.com).

Rather than tearing down a run-down building that occupied the corner lot, Leger and Wanaselja renovated it, transforming it into three lovely light-filled homes and a high-ceilinged commercial space. On the empty lot adjacent to the rehabbed building, they constructed a new building with four more condos and a ground-floor commercial unit.

The two-bedroom homes, averaging under 800 square feet each, have efficient layouts with no wasted or unusable space. The homes, says Wanaselja, "are small and dense. We're trying to fit as much housing as we can into a small area and yet we insisted on having really high ceilings and really good light and really good floor plans, so they feel a lot bigger than they are."

Homes that Are Good for People and the Planet

Green features abound: the homes are tightly built, well insulated, and designed for good daylighting and passive solar heating and cooling. Leger and Wanaselja selected healthy finishes, including plaster veneer over drywall on most walls, low- or zero-VOC paints on other walls (see box at left for more about VOCs), natural oil finishes on woodwork, and kitchen and bathroom cabinet boxes made from Medite II, a medium-density fiberboard with no added formaldehyde.

They used framing lumber certified by the Forest Stewardship Council to have come from sustainably managed forests (see page 48 for more about the FSC). Exposed wood used for interior finishes came not

A remote-controlled gate constructed of ›
Volvo tailgates opens onto the parking area.
Photo © 2005 Karl Wanaselja.

⌄ Between the buildings, a gate of salvaged retroflec-
tive street signs marks the pedestrian entrance.
Photo © 2005 Scott McGlashan.

from newly cut trees but from reclaimed sources. Old-growth Douglas fir and redwood was salvaged from the rehabbed building and reused for windowsills, walls and custom doors. Wood lath that had been covered with plaster for a century was cleaned up for use as interior siding. Columns were sculpted from salvaged Douglas fir beams.

These green strategies are commendable, but what's equally remarkable is that the Leger Wanaselja team designed and constructed this project not for a deep-pocketed, eco-minded client, but as market-rate developers. They built the nine-unit complex on speculation, confident that given a chance to buy beautiful homes that make a fearless statement about our need to be good stewards of the planet, people would jump. And jump they did. Two open houses drew 500 visitors, created a buzz of enthusiasm and landed multiple sales offers per unit at well above the asking prices. It's a new twist on the old adage: If you build it green, they will come. ❖

Back Story

Staying Light on Your Feet with Salvage

From a conversation with Cate Leger and Karl Wanaselja of Leger Wanaselja Architecture, Berkeley, California. See their Dwight Way condominium project starting on page 54 and the Jones-Elia residence on page 42.

Karl: We believe in reusing materials as much as possible to put as little pressure as possible on the production of new materials. When we are searching for a salvaged material to use, it's always critical to us that the material isn't just a decorative element. As a builder, one of the things you always need is some sort of siding material, a sheet good that you can layer in some way. One time there was this huge stack of aluminum street signs in a salvage yard and it occurred to us, why not try these things out, because they're a good material. At that time we needed a bathroom siding material that was washable up to four feet to meet the code. Why not have some fun with it? So we did this bathroom and liked it and wound up using street signs again on the next project in a different way, for the exterior siding.

Cate: I love making a really good floor plan or sequence of spaces — one that works so well, you don't even think it was designed; it just seems inevitable. That's very important to the longevity of architecture. But I also really enjoy experimenting and trying out different materials, particularly new things touted as "green" and of course things you might find in a junkyard or landfill. It's part of the fun and challenge of being a designer. All these things that you see around you — what can you do with them?

Karl: As an architect, using salvage is very hard to do on a project for a client with a builder because then there are three entities involved. Even when we're the architect, builder and client, it's still a really challenging process, but we've gotten pretty good at it internally. We're interested in throwing this extra element in because we believe it's totally worth it, both from an environmental point of view and from a design point of view.

Cate: It's really fascinating to see if there is a way to use an environmentally benign or less hazardous or less intrusive material in a way that's really creative and that can transform the material into a new use, so that you almost forget what its use was before. With our street-sign siding, when most

❮ The silvery backs of highway signs were sanded and layered for exterior siding, with sign faces peeking out underneath the bays and balconies. Photos © 2005 Karl Wanaselja.

^
License-plate siding, Telluride, Colorado. During their travels, Leger and Wanaselja get their inspiration from the resourceful ways in which people have used junk to side their buildings. Photo © 2005 Cate Leger.

people drive by, they don't even know that they were once street signs. They fit so well into their new use that you would never necessarily know, unless you look a few times, what it was before.

Karl: That idea of transformation is at the heart of our business and our philosophies and our goals. Our work as architects, as designers and as environmentalists — as artists/environmentalists — is to take these materials and transform them. We've rejected a lot. We try a lot of things before we get to the point where we'll use something. It's one of the challenges of working with salvage. You have to stay light on your feet until you find the right thing, and sometimes the waste stream doesn't supply you with that right away, and sometimes it supplies you with way too much of it and you have it sitting around for a long time and you're thinking, how am I going to use that? It's a tricky process. We're breaking new ground as developers. When was the last time you saw some wacky thing like car parts in a development?

Side Effects

Reduce, Reuse, Recycle

Once upon a time, the three Rs stood for reading, writing and 'rithmetic. Today, it's reduce, reuse and recycle. There's actually a hierarchy implied in this enviro maxim, with *reduce* as step number one. In a nutshell, lighten your footprint on the planet by using less stuff. *Reuse* and *recycle* play second and third fiddle, respectively.

Although they're often used interchangeably, reuse and recycling aren't the same. With reuse, a material isn't substantially transformed: if you turn an old colander into a witty sconce for your kitchen, you may no longer use it to drain rigatoni, but its essential colander form is still intact. That's reuse.

Recycling involves more extensive transformation. It means taking something that's considered waste, and grinding or chipping or melting it so that it can be used as raw material to make something new. Compared to reuse, recycling typically requires considerable industrial processing, with inputs of everything from energy to clean water to virgin materials.

Still, recycling and buying products made with recycled content are sound strategies for protecting the environment. When buying recycled-content products, always look for the highest *post-consumer content* available — that's the material that ends up in landfills or incinerators if it's not recycled, like newspapers, cans and bottles. Post-consumer content is different from *post-industrial* recycled content, which is manufacturing scrap that companies routinely reuse in their production processes.

Artist and furniture designer Marcia ❯ Stuermer picked up litter from the streets of San Francisco's Mission District and embedded it in a plastic resin to create her Refuge/Refuse Chaise Lounge. It's a cheeky reminder of the price we pay for the good life. Check out Stuermer's work at fossilfaux.com. Photo courtesy of Fossil Faux Studios.

ADAPTATION

Adaptive reuse is a fertile area for green-minded developers, architects, builders and homeowners. Unlike remodeling or renovation, where a residential building maintains its original function as a home, adaptive reuse refers to modifying an old building for a new purpose. A strip mall becomes a school. A bank is reborn as a community center. An icehouse becomes a home.

Of course, there's adaptive reuse and then there's *green* adaptive reuse. In truth, the difference is a matter of degrees, with green projects distinguished by a greater level of attention paid to energy efficiency, the use of reclaimed, recycled and sustainably harvested materials, and healthy indoor spaces.

Underused or abandoned commercial buildings in cities have long been prime targets for adaptive reuse, providing a double bang for the buck: the building and all the resources that went into constructing it don't go to waste, and the neighborhood gets a jolt of revitalization. (This can be a mixed blessing if gentrification elbows long-time residents from their community.)

Historic preservation is another benefit of adaptive reuse. Reusing a time-worn building, even if only the exterior remains intact while the interior is reconfigured, preserves a piece of our community's past, and with it an inkling of knowledge about who lived and worked, raised families and grew old in our neighborhoods.

In the chapter "Turning Koo's Corner," we see loft homes born from an auto services garage, revitalizing a city corner while retaining an echo of the property's past. Naturally this transformation is just the beginning of the green story: the homes were also designed to be energy efficient and healthy, with recycled and salvaged materials used throughout.

In "A Very Cool Icehouse," we meet a Brooklyn couple who bought a run-down brick building, originally built for ice storage, and converted it into apartments. Not content with a conventional adaptation, they went for the green, from remilling and reusing the structure's floorboards and beams to topping the building with a living roof and solar-electric panels.

Finally, the chapter "What Goes Around Comes Around" presents a unique angle on adaptive reuse. Instead of transforming an old building, the owner and his design and construction team transformed surplus shipping containers — metal structures originally used to transport cargo — into a home that dramatically blends old and new.

© 2005 Laurie Lambrecht (page 76)

© 2005 Kristopher Grunert

KOD'S
AUTO SERVICE

OPEN

The exterior siding of the townhouses is a fiber-cement product; it earns green accolades because it's noncombustible, low maintenance and considered to be very durable.

Turning Koo's Corner

Where: Vancouver, British Columbia

Developer/Green Building Consultant: reSource Rethinking Building, Inc.
Rethinkingbuilding.com
604.678.9024

Architect: Hotson Bakker Boniface Haden Architects

General Contractor: Timberland Homes

Photographer: Kristopher Grunert

Transforming an Auto Repair Shop into City Homes

Many developers wouldn't have given a second thought to bulldozing the old Koo's Auto Service building in Vancouver's Strathcona neighborhood. On the surface, little distinguished the garage, which dated to the 1940s. Fortunately when proprietor Gordy Koo retired, he sold the 6,000-square-foot property not just to any buyer but to a green developer.

Instead of carting Koo's garage off to a landfill, developer Robert Brown, working with green building consultant Heather Tremain* and architect Bruce Haden, decided to save the structure and convert it into two loft-style homes. On the property's south side, on what was once the garage's parking lot, they built four more homes.

Reusing the Koo's building accrued social as well as environmental benefits: the garage had contributed to Strathcona's sense of place, so by preserving an echo of it, the community retains a connection to its

< On the south end of the property (right), the developer sited three new townhouses, giving them peaked roofs and front porches to complement the neighborhood's older homes. A more modern-looking glass-fronted townhouse creates a transition between the converted garage and the townhouses. Inset: the original Koo's garage.

* Brown's company, Chesterman Property Group, developed the project. Brown and Tremain are now partners in the green building consulting company, reSource Rethinking Building, Inc., located in Vancouver. They specialize in providing building owners and real estate developers with expertise and information to create healthy and environmentally friendly buildings. More: rethinkingbuilding.com.

The old garage before being transformed into loft homes. A high ceiling and open floor area made the timber-frame garage a good candidate for adaptive reuse.

In the new townhouses, floorboards were milled from glulams reclaimed from a deconstructed commercial building. Glulam, an abbreviation of "glued laminated" timber, is an engineered wood product made of layers of wood bound with an adhesive and formed into large structural beams. >

REUSE RECAP

- ❏ Reuse of auto service building and remediation of contaminated brownfield (oil-soaked soil replaced)
- ❏ Reuse or recycling of 80 percent of construction and demolition waste
- ❏ Use of reclaimed wood for flooring, stairs, cabinets and more
- ❏ Use of reclaimed lumber for more than 50 percent of framing
- ❏ Reuse of salvaged utility poles for fences and trellises
- ❏ Fifty percent recycled fly ash used in poured concrete

MORE GREEN STRATEGIES

- ❏ High-density urban infill site, close to downtown, transit and neighborhood services
- ❏ Solar hot-water systems in two units; others pre-plumbed for future installation
- ❏ Heat-recovery ventilation system that filters incoming fresh air and recaptures heat from exhaust air
- ❏ Energy Star appliances
- ❏ Low-VOC paints and sealants
- ❏ Carpets have Carpet and Rug Institute's Green Label, indicating reduced chemical offgassing
- ❏ Cabinet boxes made of composite board with no added urea formaldehyde
- ❏ Permeable paving in driveway areas provides continuous grass strip along sidewalk to reduce rainwater runoff into sewers while providing hard surface for driving
- ❏ Drought-tolerant landscaping; no permanent irrigation system

history. Tearing it down would have meant another stroke of the development eraser blanking out the neighborhood's roots.

Koo's Corner, as the development is named in honor of the original proprietor, is a compact, stylish urban compound, with six units ranging from 720 to 1,200 square feet. The steeply pitched roofs of the three new townhouses on the south end evoke the neighbor-hood's older row houses. A glass-fronted two-level home with a roof deck bridges the townhouses and the lofts in the old garage. This mélange of styles suits Strathcona to a T. As Vancouver's oldest residential neighborhood, once known as the East End, Strathcona has been home to successive waves of immigrants. Today it's a lively community with a diverse population and an eclectic mix of building types, from corner stores and commercial buildings to apartment houses, restored Queen Anne Victorians, and modest cottages on narrow lots.

City Style, Healthy Homes

Brown and Tremain developed Koo's Corner as a market-rate project, and all the homes sold out while still under construction (Tremain purchased one and architect Haden bought another). In keeping with the developer's mission to create "beautiful, healthy and sustain-able" housing, the buildings were designed with high ceilings, large windows and skylights to give the small homes a spacious feel, and with contemporary finishes such as glass awnings and concrete floors and counters.

< High ceilings and copious daylight help make these small homes live larger.

Inside Scoop

Brownfields: Reclaiming Polluted Properties

The U.S. Environmental Protection Agency (EPA) defines a brownfield as "a property, the expansion, redevelopment, or reuse of which may be complicated by the presence or potential presence of a hazardous substance, pollutant, or contaminant." Contaminants may include petrochemicals, like the oil-soaked soil at Koo's Corner, heavy metals in the soil or groundwater, asbestos in existing structures on the site, and a host of other hazardous pollutants.

The EPA estimates that there are more than 450,000 brownfields in the United States, in rural and suburban areas as well as industrialized urban zones. Cleaning up and redeveloping these contaminated sites is an important green-building strategy that improves the environment and reduces pressure to develop farmlands and wildlands.

To encourage the remediation of brownfields, city, state and federal regulators have passed laws that protect developers from future liability once specified clean-up activities take place, and have made available grants, tax breaks and other financial incentives. Find out more at the EPA's brownfields Web site: epa.gov/brownfields.

While contemporary style catches the eye, eco-friendly features do their work behind the scenes. Fiberglass wall insulation with 60 to 80 percent recycled content, installed at a thickness that exceeds local building-code requirements, helps keep the homes comfortable and utility bills low. In the loft units, high-efficiency gas water heaters supply the hot-water taps and a radiant-floor heating system. One home was built with solar hot-water panels on its roof. Tremain notes that four of the other units were pre-plumbed so that the homeowners could add solar hot water in the future without the hassle or expense of penetrating the roof or walls. And in fact, one of the homeowners did later add a solar hot-water collector.

The energy-efficient homes were also designed with indoor air quality in mind. Brown and Tremain chose low-emitting cabinets, paints and finishes that don't offgas unhealthy levels of VOCs (see page 60 for more about VOCs). Good air circulation is provided by operable windows placed high on the wall (to create airflow through what's known as stack ventilation), ceiling fans and heat-recovery ventilation systems.

From the reused shell of the old garage to details like fencing made from salvaged utility poles, Koo's Corner shows us a way to honor the old while making room for the new. ❖

^
Bathroom vanities are simple and stylish concrete. The vanity base and shelves are reclaimed fir. Photo courtesy of reSource Rethinking Building, Inc.

Kitchen-cabinet doors are solid fir reclaimed from beams that were once part of the Steveston Cannery on British Columbia's Fraser River. All composite board used in the homes, including the cabinet boxes, has no added urea formaldehyde. Photo courtesy of reSource Rethinking Building, Inc. >

© 2005 Alan Shortall

A historic Elks Lodge in Litchfield, Illinois, was restored and converted into twenty-seven affordable-rate apartments.

Side Effects

Public Good: Historic Preservation, Affordable Housing and Green Building

"If you've got it, you should use it," says Doug Farr, founding principal of Chicago's Farr Associates, an architecture, planning and historic preservation firm committed to sustainable design. He's referring not merely to the historic value of an old building but also to its embodied energy — "the idea that you built something once and it took some effort and resources to do so."

Much of Farr Associates' work is on the scale of entire neighborhoods and towns, but they also renew individual buildings, with an eye toward preserving architectural and historic integrity while adapting the building to changing needs. In the mid-1990s, Farr happened upon a dilapidated Elks Lodge in the small town of Litchfield, Illinois, on historic Route 66. Built in 1923, the once-grand lodge had been a vacant white elephant for years, and a leaking roof had wrought considerable interior damage.

To the untrained eye the building was on the brink of ruin. But Farr, calling the steel-framed structure "bomb-proof," says "it was built well the first time, so even as it went into disuse and even prolonged vacancy," it still had reuse potential.

Farr Associates assisted the building owner with obtaining double tax credits for affordable housing and historic rehabilitation, and set to work on plans for adapting the lodge into twenty-seven affordable-rate rental apartments. "We emphasized energy efficiency and insulated the heck out of it," Farr says, using blown-in cellulose insulation made from recycled newspapers. Skylights with deep shafts were

In its heyday, the lodge boasted a swimming pool and bowling alley > in the basement. Farr Associates salvaged the bowling lane during the renovation; a section of it now serves as a conference table in their Chicago office. Note the fault line at the near end of the table.

added to bring daylight to the corridors on the third and fourth floors, in the space once occupied by a ballroom.

In addition to creating much-needed affordable housing and giving new life to a decaying building, the project brought renewed vitality to Litchfield's small downtown. Learn more about Farr Associates' work at farrside.com.

The building was a white elephant, with graffiti and water damage marring the interior.
∨

Courtesy of Farr Associates

The fireplace and many other details were painstakingly restored.
∨

© 2005 Alan Shortall

A ballroom occupied the top floor of the three-story lodge. Farr Associates designed a fourth floor of apartments that was inserted into the ballroom volume, with new skylights to illuminate the interior.
∨

© 2005 Alan Shortall

A new penthouse and stairwell wrap around the original brick building. The elevated Franklin Avenue Shuttle rolls by at regular intervals.

A Very Cool Icehouse

Where: Brooklyn, New York

Designer: Benton Brown

Owner/Builder: Susan Boyle and Benton Brown
Big Sue, Inc.
bigsuellc@verizon.net
718.857.2717

Photographers: Laurie Lambrecht, Benton Brown, Susan Boyle

An Artist and an Environmentalist Transform a Derelict Brooklyn Warehouse

Subway cars rattle along an elevated track outside Susan Boyle and Benton Brown's windows, drowning out their voices every now and then as we talk on the phone. The noise is so evocative of New York and the lives of a young couple living in a souped-up warehouse that I wonder for a split second if it's for real. But as I discovered then and later when we meet in person, there's nothing false about Boyle and Brown, both in their early thirties, or the sturdily handsome live/work building they've rehabbed in Brooklyn's Crown Heights neighborhood.

The story of how they wound up living in a converted icehouse reads like a classic New York tale with a twenty-first-century twist. Benton Brown, a sculptor, and his wife, Susan Boyle, were looking for an old building to renovate that would be large enough to live in and accommodate Brown's welding and shop equipment. Not an easy mission in space-starved New York. And Boyle, whose background is in environmental work for a nonprofit group,

The icehouse, before and after transformation into apartments. The interior was gutted and reinforced with structural steel and poured concrete. A new stairwell was added at back, as well as a penthouse. Photos © 2005 Benton Brown.

It takes vision and pluck to transform a derelict, pigeon-infested building into attractive apartments. The oak flooring, likely added in the 1950s when the two-story icehouse was converted into a four-story warehouse, seemed hopelessly decrepit. Big Sue's crew pried it up, remilled much of it, and reused it for interior door frames and other trim.

Brown and Boyle's own loft occupies the original building's top floor and the new penthouse. Tall windows allow daylight to reach deep into the space. Ceiling heights in the apartments range from thirteen to eighteen feet. The stair treads are remilled beams from the original structure.

REUSE RECAP

- Conversion of a nineteenth-century brewery building into six apartments and an artist's studio
- Deconstruction of interior and extensive reuse of wood beams and floors
- Salvaged pedestal sinks and claw-foot bathtubs
- Reused interior doors; new front door made from salvaged beams
- Use of salvaged workers' lockers for linen cabinets and storage
- New poured concrete with 30 to 40 percent recycled fly ash content

MORE GREEN STRATEGIES

- Urban site with easy access to public transit
- 7.2-kilowatt solar-electric array, grid tied with no battery backup
- Vegetated roof
- Rain barrels to collect water for roof irrigation
- No air-conditioning; cross ventilation, ceiling and in-wall fans, and building's significant thermal mass for cooling.
- Highly efficient condensing boilers and hydronic radiant-floor heating system
- Energy Star appliances

was eager to get hands-on experience with the sustainable building practices and technologies she'd been learning about over the years.

A Monster of a Building at an Incredible Price

Finding the right building took an enterprising spirit and perseverance. "We probably searched for two years," Brown recalls, "riding our bikes around in different neighborhoods, looking for abandoned buildings. Most of the time we were just a month behind some broker, somebody that had snatched it up. It was a frustrating search."

One day, when looking at another property in northern Crown Heights, a working-class neighborhood south of Bedford Stuyvesant and east of Prospect Heights, they chanced upon what a real estate broker referred to as a "monster of a building" at "an incredible price."

Looking beyond the graffiti-strewn façade, the couple was immediately drawn to the chunky 14,000-square-foot brick building that was constructed sometime during the second half of the 1800s as the Nassau Brewery's icehouse. It was the right size to meet their own needs as well as accommodating several income-producing rental apartments. And while it had been neglected for years, the ground floor occupied by a moving company but the upper floors inhabited only by rats and pigeons, the location suited the couple — it's a slightly gritty area on the margin between commercial and residential zones.

‹ In the kitchen area, an eleven-by-five-foot butcher-block island on a steel frame was assembled by Big Sue's crew from end-grain scraps of wood left over during construction.

© 2005 Benton Brown

The new hydronic radiant-floor heating system includes 16,000 linear feet of tubing throughout the building. In Brown and Boyle's own two-story, 3,000-square-foot apartment, shown here before the concrete floors were poured, twelve separate zones allow for temperature control. The building, with its two-foot-thick masonry walls, stays comfortable in the summer without air-conditioning. "We keep the transoms open all the time in the summer, and we have great cross ventilation," Boyle says. "We've also got ceiling fans in all the units. To me, it's perfect. I'm not a big fan of air-conditioning for a lot of reasons."

The problem was, the owner wouldn't sell just the icehouse. A buyer would have to take all seven of his dilapidated buildings — 135,000 square feet sprawling over three adjacent tax lots. That was a bigger bite of a white elephant than Brown or Boyle intended to chew, but they'd already fallen hard for that redbrick icehouse with its two-foot-thick walls, so they plunged in. Brown recalls, "We started trying to put together some kind of development package to get people interested so we could possibly buy it. It was huge — much bigger than we were thinking."

Boyle adds that ideally they would have kept all the buildings "because they're all so funky and so beautiful in their own kind of rat-infested way."

But economic reality dictated that they present potential investors — a group of family and friends — with a plan to buy and then quickly sell off two of the three lots in order to finance the redevelopment of the two buildings on the remaining lot, the icehouse and an adjacent 46,000-square-foot brick warehouse. The couple formed a general contracting company, Big Sue, Inc. — named after Susan Boyle, who stands about

The bookshelves separating the office and sitting ❯
area are reclaimed wood from the original structure.
Used office furniture is right at home here.

Inside Scoop

Old Stuff to Be Wary Of

Think twice before snapping up what may seem like a bargain at your local junkyard. Some salvaged materials contain hazardous chemicals or don't perform as well as their new counterparts. Items to watch out for include:

❑ *Single-pane windows and glass doors.* These are typically half as energy efficient as new double-pane products, and not allowed by energy codes in many regions. Unless you live in a very mild climate, consider using them where energy efficiency isn't a concern, such as interior partitions between rooms (your local building code may require safety glass in some situations; retrofit films are available to help provide shatter resistance).

❑ *Old toilets.* Don't buy them. Today's new toilets use 1.6 gallons per flush or less. Most old toilets use four or more gallons per flush and don't meet local building codes.

❑ *Pressure-treated salvaged wood.* Since January 2004, the treated wood industry has voluntarily phased out most uses of wood treated with chromated copper arsenate (CCA) preservatives because of health concerns related to arsenic exposure. If your project requires pressure-treated wood, seek out one of the newer, safer alternatives. The Healthy Building Network has information at healthybuilding.net.

❑ *Bricks.* Before World War I, brick walls were built with a lime-based mortar that's relatively easy to chisel off when salvaging bricks. Modern cement-based mortars are much

five-foot-four — and within a year managed to sell the five unneeded properties to a nonprofit arts organization that plans to develop them into affordable housing for artists.

From Icehouse to Apartment House, Salvage Style

Brown is an artist, not an architect or builder by trade, but he did have some prior construction experience, including converting a leased, 10,000-square-foot building, also in Brooklyn, into four lofts, one of which he and Boyle lived in for about five years. After obtaining variances to convert the icehouse to residential use, Brown and Boyle set to work on rehabbing it (work on the adjacent warehouse will happen in a later phase). Brown drew up plans for converting the building into six apartments — a two-level, 3,000-square-foot loft for themselves and five rental units ranging from 1,100 to 1,450 square feet — and a large workshop for Brown on the ground floor. Boyle and Brown shared general contracting duties and did much of the labor themselves with a small crew of friends and a few workers hired from the moving and storage company that previously operated out of some of the buildings on the site.

As if rehabbing a rundown building wasn't ambitious enough, the couple set out to reuse as much of the stuff they were stripping out of the building as possible. It wasn't merely a matter of doing good for the planet. Much of the material was high quality, and what's more, reuse aligned with their appreciation for the good looks of exposed brick, steel, concrete and other rugged materials.

The couple reused not just the building's skeleton but also the materials they pulled out when gutting the interior, including about 7,000 square feet of wood floors as well as the hefty floor joists. Their crew remilled forty wood beams, turning them into ten-inch-wide floorboards, shelves, stair treads, windowsills, molding and a large carriage house–style front door. The original oak floorboards, too decrepit to reuse as flooring, were planed and turned into door frames and other trim. Interior doors were stripped, refinished and rehung.

Owning an empty warehouse adjacent to the icehouse proved to be the linchpin in their ability to work successfully with reclaimed materials. "That larger building enabled us to have all this storage space," Boyle explains, "so we used the ground floor as a staging area" for the loads of salvageable wood and brick Big Sue's crew hauled out of the icehouse, and as a temporary shop for welding and woodworking. "By no means did we have the foresight to figure that out," she says, laughing, "but it fell into place and it was so critical." Boyle and Brown estimate that they were able to reuse about 75 percent of the material that came out of the demolition process.

All that storage space also came in handy for other bulky salvaged goods. A local salvage dealer who got wind of the couple's interest in cool old stuff would swing by regularly, his truck loaded with claw-foot tubs, pedestal sinks and other treasures picked up on his rounds. Boyle recalls that at one point they had thirty claw-foot tubs in their storage area. "We ended up picking the best ones out of the thirty and then he took the rest back. It was a pretty perfect arrangement."

harder and can be a real bear to scrape off — the brick itself often breaks before the mortar does. Jennifer Corson, author of *The Resourceful Renovator,* cautions that some salvaged bricks are not appropriate for structural uses, but that it can be difficult for the untrained eye to distinguish between load-bearing and non-load-bearing bricks. Hire an experienced brick mason or structural engineer to inspect reclaimed bricks before using them for exterior veneer, fireplaces or in a load-bearing capacity. Also check local building codes to ensure that using salvaged brick is permitted. Never sandblast old brick — besides ruining its appearance, you can damage its hard surface and expose the brick to weather damage.

❏ *Lead-based paint.* Lead was a common additive to many oil-based paints before 1978, and it can pose a serious health risk, particularly for children, if paint chips are ingested or paint dust inhaled. Be cautious when working with salvaged windows, doors or other painted objects. If lead is suspected but the paint is in good condition, you can seal it with a liquid coating called paint encapsulant. Some encapsulants include a nontoxic but bitter ingredient to discourage little tykes from chewing on the stuff. Don't use heat guns to remove lead-based paint; only use a mechanical sander if it has a HEPA (high-efficiency particulate air) filter. Seattle's Environmental Home Center has good information about less toxic gel-based paint strippers: environmentalhomecenter.com. For information about safe practices for dealing with lead-based paint, go to the U.S. Environmental Protection Agency Web site (epa.gov/lead) or call their hotline at 800-424-LEAD.

A New Beginning for an Old Building

Brown's design honors the building's original workhorse spirit, with exposed brick walls, high ceilings and oversized windows that flood the interior with daylight. When the couple selected new rather than reclaimed materials and products, they did so with an eye to high performance, durability, energy efficiency and unassuming good looks.

Four years from when they first set eyes on the building, the rehab was complete and all units rented, with tenants ensconced in their new-old homes. The sturdy icehouse that attracted Brown and Boyle hasn't been lost in the transformation. "People are pretty excited about the space," Boyle says. "The apartments are very simple, they're not at all luxurious or fancy units, but people really seem to like the simplicity of it. And there's also excitement about the idea of a green building. It's gratifying." ❖

© 2005 Laurie Lambrecht

For the penthouse, new wood flooring was milled from original beams removed when Big Sue's crew gutted the building. "We took all this lumber out," Brown says, "and then we basically put it all back in – minus a lot of sawdust." Although the wood was essentially free, "I wouldn't say that making the flooring was such a cost-saving process," he cautions. "We only did about 1,000 square feet of flooring, but it used up a lot of the lumber and was very time-consuming.

< With few interior walls, areas can be reconfigured to meet changing needs. All the new concrete used in the project contains 30 to 40 percent recycled fly ash. (For more about fly ash, see page 134.) Windowsills are milled from beams removed from the building.

Back Story

Green-It-Yourself Starts with Doing Your Homework

Ever dream of converting a white elephant of a building into a green home? Where would you start? Some people hire architects or builders with green expertise to lead them through the process. But Susan Boyle and Benton Brown took it upon themselves to learn the ins-and-outs and ups-and-downs of designing and building green. Here's a taste of how and why they did it:

"My background is as an environmentalist working for a nonprofit," Boyle explains. "So I was really committed and excited about learning more about green building and technologies and things like a green roof and solar, and even things that we didn't necessarily do but I wanted to find out more about, like researching wind power."

She and Brown conducted much of their research on the Internet, and stocked up on books about construction. One of their favorite publications is *Environmental Building News,* a monthly newsletter that's free of advertising and, as Boyle notes, "is really honest about things" (buildinggreen.com).

The couple also took advantage of local events and classes. "We found out about conferences," Boyle recalls, "and really tried to go and talk to people as much as possible. Earth Pledge had a green roofs conference that I found really useful, and we met our source for plants there.* We took a solar installation class where we ended up meeting the person we hired to do the solar installation, but we also educated ourselves about it so we weren't just going into it blindly."

© 2005 Laurie Lambrecht

^
On top of Brown and Boyle's building, layers of impermeable substrate, lightweight planting medium, and hardy plants cover 2,300 square feet of roof. Today's green roofs are a new take on an old idea. In the summer, green roofs (also called vegetated or living roofs) help reduce ambient air temperatures in cities and slow the flow of storm water into sewers. They prolong the life of the roof, insulate the building and restore a bit of nature to a neighborhood where virtually every inch of land is developed. This photo was taken ten months after planting the roof with sedum, lavender and chives. Over time, the plants will spread to provide much denser coverage.

* Through its Green Roofs Initiative, the nonprofit organization Earth Pledge is working "to lower New York City's ambient air temperature and prevent pollution in its waterways by creating citywide green roof infrastructure." Go to earthpledge.org.

To heat the building, the couple opted for a radiant system that circulates hot water within tubing embedded in the concrete floor. Radiant systems are particularly effective for heating large volumes of space because they warm people and objects rather than air.* "I'm a little bit crazy about heating systems," says Brown, "so I really wanted to research all of that in a big way. We had a mechanical engineer and it was constant arguing about what was the right thing to do. We tried to learn as much as we could about different heating systems and pumps and different loops, and what's the best for hot water. Our boilers we found online, researching different kinds of super-efficient boilers."

In addition to energy efficiency, durability was a high priority. "We always joked about how we wanted something that was going to last 300 years," Brown says, laughing. "Every time we would install something we would always say, 'Oka-a-ay, I'm not sure if that's going to make it 300 years!'"

Brown and Boyle have registered their building with the U.S. Green Building Council's LEED Green Building Rating System, and hope to achieve certification in 2005. For more about LEED, see page 31.

© 2005 Susan Boyle

Susan Boyle and Benton Brown on the roof of their renovated building. ❯ They're sitting on a 7.2-kilowatt "peel and stick" solar-electric array that fits between a metal roof's standing seams. The laminate system is called Uni-Solar; check it out at smartroofsolar.com.

* If you're contemplating adding radiant-floor heat to an existing building, keep in mind that the tubing can raise the floor level, so you need adequate ceiling height. Also, if the building has ducts for central air-conditioning, it will be much less expensive to use those for heating, too, rather than add a separate system for radiant-floor heating.

© 2005 Maria Ancona

The owner divided a sprawling scrap yard to build a modern house out of old junk. The house sits at the back of the lot and is approached through a tropical garden.

What Goes Around Comes Around

Where: Los Angeles, California

Architect: Office of Mobile Design
Venice, California
310.439.1129
designmobile.com

Owner/Creative Director/General Contractor: Richard Carlson

Interior design: David Mocarski

Landscape design: James Stone

Photographer: Undine Pröhl

< Humble materials meet high design in this loft-like house built of scrapped shipping containers and other industrial detritus.

Humble Cargo Containers Meet High Style

"How the old and new, the high and the low come together" fires up architect Jennifer Siegal's imagination. "Something that is old and weathered can be up against something that is new and shiny," she says. "They form a relationship, kind of a co-arising of the two materials, so that when the two things come together they're actually stronger than the single unit."

Siegal, founder and principal of the Office of Mobile Design (OMD), has a flair for artfully juxtaposing old and new. At the Seatrain residence, a 3,000-square-foot house she designed with developer Richard Carlson, time-worn wooden beams and metal shipping containers combine with gleaming walls of glass to create a dramatic dwelling in an industrial area near downtown Los Angeles. Completed in 2003, this contemporary home and its oasis-like garden take up one side of the 10,000-square-foot

A lush garden provides a counterpoint to the industrial salvage used to build the home.

REUSE RECAP

❏ Surplus shipping containers transformed into a modern home

❏ Scrapped grain trailers repurposed as koi ponds

❏ Salvaged steel beams

❏ Reclaimed Douglas fir roof joists

MORE GREEN STRATEGIES

❏ Durable, low-maintenance materials

❏ Urban infill site

"I used to see a large box by the railroad, six feet long by three wide, in which the laborers locked up their tools at night; and it suggested to me that every man who was hard pushed might get such a one for a dollar, and, having bored a few auger holes in it, to admit the air at least, get into it when it rained and at night, and hook down the lid, and so have freedom in his love, and in his soul be free."

—Henry David Thoreau, *Walden*

Inside and out, two open-topped grain trailers were converted into koi ponds.

lot where the Carlson family's building demolition company, Carlson Industries, stockpiles salvaged materials.

Cargo Containers Come Home at Last

Much of Seatrain was built with junk from Carlson's scrap yard, including four abandoned forty-foot-long containers, stacked two high on either side of the house. By design, cargo containers are nomadic, hauled around the globe by train, truck and ship, but eventually many come to rest in railroad yards or junkyards. People like Carlson and Siegal look at those hulking metal shells and see an enticing tabula rasa.

"The shipping containers were sitting there. We never moved them. We built the house around them or with them in mind," Siegal says of the structures, two of which are aluminum-clad and two steel. "All we ended up doing was carving the ground around them, and carving into them, and wrapping materials around and on top of them."

Each eight-foot-wide container defines a semi-separate zone in the home. On the east side, the lower container serves as a media room, while above it another container houses the master bedroom, which projects out into the garden. On the opposite side of the house, the downstairs container holds a guest bath, laundry and mechanical room, while upstairs a container with one side peeled off provides dining and office space overlooking the living area below.

< A waterfall flows over stacked flagstones. Over the pond, a tempered glass bridge demarcates the public and more private areas of the house.

Daylight pours into the home through a wall of glass facing the garden.

Salvaged steel beams span the expanse between the two sets of containers, creating a high-ceilinged core for the kitchen and main living area. "It's a loft, essentially," Siegal says. "There are distinct zones but they all open onto each other."

In the main living area and the garden, two open-topped grain trailers, each five feet deep, were given new life as koi ponds. "You see them going down the freeway filled with oranges or grain," Siegal says of the trailers. "They're called fast pushers. When one end opens up it's able to pour its load out. We also had those on the site. We rearranged them, built up the ground plane around one and outside we sunk it into the ground."

Collaboration, Adaptation and Imagination

Although the house wasn't envisioned initially as a green building, Siegal's interest in sustainable architecture "was able to soak into the project," she says. The use of surplus shipping containers and grain trailers certainly gives the project bragging rights in the world of green design. "The major bones in the structure of the building were

Cargo containers stacked two high on opposite sides of the ❯ house are bridged by a roof supported by salvaged steel beams and reclaimed Douglas fir joists. Ribbed steel B-decking serves as the ceiling and roof, with foam insulation between.

all salvaged," Siegal points out, including the Douglas fir joists in the ceiling and the steel beams that span the roof.

Carlson and Siegal collaborated closely on the project with many other designers and fabricators, most of whom had at some point lived or worked across the street at the Brewery, another of Carlson's projects. In the 1980s, he transformed this former Pabst Blue Ribbon facility into a 300-unit live/work complex for artists.*

"It was very much like a communal project," Siegal says of Seatrain's design and construction process. "While we had an overriding blueprint or theme or structure, when we were out on the site, we were making decisions and transforming things. If all of a sudden we noticed a view that we didn't see before, we'd cut a window. It wasn't like we were forcing a plan upon something. It was much more of a fluid, graceful collaboration."

Adapting shipping containers or other structures not originally intended as homes isn't for the faint of heart. "These are unusual projects," Siegal notes. "They don't take traditional paths. You need to have an adventurous spirit. You need to have a lot of trust in yourself and the people you're working with."

* Artists living and working at the Brewery open their studios to the
public twice a year. It's a great opportunity to check out what's
billed as "the world's largest art colony." Go to breweryartwalk.com.

The master bedroom cantilevers over
the main living area and the garden.

Inside Scoop

Building with Containers

Surplus shipping containers have long served as sturdy storage units, and even as dwellings in some parts of the world, particularly developing nations. In the United States and other affluent countries, there's been a recent surge of interest in adapting these versatile structures for residential use.

What's the appeal? There's something archetypal about these stripped-down boxes; perhaps the sight of an industrial zone with colorful containers stacked five high stirs up memories of playing with blocks. Containers are modular, customizable, stackable, strong and, thanks to a glut in some regions, relatively inexpensive. A used but still usable container can sometimes be had for as little as $2,000.

But don't expect smooth sailing if you're hankering after a container cottage of your own. After all, they are narrow, windowless boxes designed to hold cargo, not people. They come in lengths of twenty or forty feet, which may sound commodious, but the standard eight-foot width and eight-and-a-half-foot height can make claustrophobics shudder.

(Continued on page 102.)

It also helps to have an owner who is an experienced builder and developer. "He built the Brewery," Siegal says of Carlson. "He knows what he's doing."

Part of the thrill of building with salvage is the lure of heading into uncharted territory. "Sometimes it's easier to work if there's a set of rules and you're trying to break the rules, rather than if it's just a white page and there's no mark on that page," Siegal says. The challenge of salvaged materials "is in how far you can stretch your imagination." ❖

Unassuming materials – corrugated steel, cargo containers, salvaged wood joists – set the stage for sleek modern furnishings. ❯

(Continued from page 100.)

Built to withstand rough handling, a typical container has a steel frame, a skin of aluminum or steel, and plank or plywood floors. As with all salvage, there's no guidebook for building with containers. Expect to face challenges from local building officials, and potential difficulties in finding contractors willing to tackle the project if you aren't building it yourself. Be sure to consult with a structural engineer, especially if you plan to stack or cut into the containers; opening up the steel or aluminum sides may compromise their structural integrity.

If you're interested in container dwellings, check out the recent crop of intriguing projects. Architect Adam Kalkin converted a container into exhibition space for Vermont's Shelburne Museum, and has developed container house designs (architectureandhygiene.com). New York City's LOT-EK (lot-ek.com) has inventive ideas for residential and commercial spaces using shipping containers. In London's Docklands, Container City is an artists' live/work development made of surplus cargo containers (containercity.com). Australian architect Sean Godsell's Future Shack is a prototype for relocatable emergency housing made from recycled shipping containers (seangodsell.com).

∧
< The Eco Lab, a portable classroom where schoolchildren learn about environmental protection. Photos © 2005 Benny Chan, Fotoworks.

Back Story

Plug & Play from the Office of Mobile Design

With the Seatrain house, Jennifer Siegal and her collaborators transformed once-mobile structures — surplus shipping containers and grain trailers — into a building that's decidedly rooted in place. "These building materials that lived a very mobile, nomadic life have come to rest momentarily, like an old train yard," Siegal says. "They are finding their moment of stasis."

The Portable Construction Training Center, ➤
or PCTC, a training center where workers
learn the basic construction trades. Photos
© 2005 Benny Chan, Fotoworks.

The solidity of Seatrain notwithstanding, these days Siegal's interests have taken her into the realm of what she calls "non-permanently sited structures." In her book *Mobile: The Art of Portable Architecture* she writes, "While architecture's purpose remains constant — providing shelter from the natural elements and community among its inhabitants — mobile and portable structures herald the dawn of the age of new nomadism."

Fueled by converging interests in mobility, technology, sustainability and community, Siegal undertakes projects ranging from prefab houses to traveling classrooms. Her firm, the Office of Mobile Design (OMD)* is in the vanguard of a burgeoning interest in prefab — a peppy moniker for modular homes that are built in a factory and transported as more-or-less whole units to the homeowner's property. Stereotypes about manufactured housing persist — think of the disdain projected by the term "trailer trash." But today a number of trendsetting architects, including Siegal, are working to redefine our notions of the old "mobile" home by marketing designs that emphasize flexibility, comfort and modern style.

Meanwhile, at Woodbury University in Los Angeles, where she is a professor of architecture, Siegal's students have designed and built mobile "hands-on learning environments" made from "all recycled, found and donated materials," including salvage donated by Carlson Industries. In collaboration with the nonprofit Hollywood Beautification Team, Siegal's students transformed an eight-by-thirty-five-foot furniture-moving trailer into the Eco Lab, a mobile classroom that traveled around Los Angeles County, providing a place for K–12 school students to learn about the life-cycle of a tree and the value of environmental protection.

Siegal's students also designed and built the Portable Construction Training Center, or PCTC, for the Venice Community Housing Corporation, a nonprofit organization that builds housing for

people with low incomes. Formerly an old manufactured house, it's now a mobile fourteen-by-sixty-five-foot classroom with individual bays where student trainees get hands-on experience with construction skills. "They can practice things and tear it out," Siegal says. "They learn how to plumb a sink, and then they'll pull that out and the next person will do it."

The Eco Lab and PCTC may seem worlds apart from the Seatrain house, but they share common roots: teams of designers and builders took humble materials that happened to be at hand and transformed them into engaging places for living, working and learning.

* OMD has developed a number of prefab designs including Portable House, a sleek, flexible structure that's intended to be more affordable than a custom-designed home and more attractive than conventional manufactured housing, and Swellhouse, a custom house built of prefabricated modular components. Check them out at designmobile.com. Another attractive, modern prefab house is architect Michelle Kaufmann's Glidehouse (glidehouse.com). **Prefab,** a book by Bryan Burkhart and Allison Arieff, takes a look at more than twenty-five prefab designs. Arieff is editor-in-chief of **Dwell** magazine (dwellmag.com), which tracks trends in modern design, including prefab housing.

NEW CONSTRUCTION

Whether you use your own hands or hire pros, building a new house offers an unsurpassed opportunity to make it green from the get-go.

A home's largest environmental impact stems from the amount of energy it uses year after year, so don't miss this chance to make it as energy efficient as possible. Now's the time to think about designing for passive solar heating and daylighting, to look for opportunities to incorporate renewable-energy technologies like photovoltaics and solar hot-water systems, to create a tight building envelope that resists moisture and air infiltration, and to insulate the heck out of the place.

The decisions you make when planning your new house will affect not just your own experience of living in it but the experience of everyone who lives in it after you. So now is also the time to think about designing for "long life, loose fit" — in other words, create a house that can be readily reconfigured as your needs evolve (the size of your household grows or shrinks, for example, or your physical abilities change as you age) and that can be easily adapted by future occupants. A home that's built today with a loose fit is more likely to remain functional and loved for generations, and less likely to wind up demolished and trucked off to a landfill.

Building a new house uses vast amounts of materials: wood, stone, windows, roofing, insulation, building paper, drywall, tiles, piping, wiring, paint and more. Obviously, the bigger the house, the more stuff goes into building it, so for the sake of the environment it's important to be mindful of square footage. But reducing a home's size isn't the only path to conserving natural resources. Even in brand-new homes, reuse can play a starring role.

In the chapter "Beauty & Brains," a homeowner, her architect and builder cut back on new resources by incorporating not just reclaimed wood but more unusual salvage such as railroad tracks, wheels from ore-mining carts, and Piper Cherokee airplane flaps.

In "Putting It Back Together," two architect-builders dismantle a fifty-year-old home that had seen better days and put it back together as a new house that blends bold design with smart green building strategies.

A new house needn't be extravagant, as we see in "Back to Basics," which features a weekend house built of straw bales. To some people, recycling strategies like building with straw bales or mixing fly ash in concrete may sound experimental. But the owner of this home knows that these construction techniques work well and do good.

Finally, in "Principles into Practice," reclaimed wood and other salvaged materials set the stage for a family home that celebrates the best of today's ecological design.

Beauty & Brains

Where: Gardnerville, Nevada

Architect: Arkin Tilt Architects
Berkeley, California
510.528.9830
arkintilt.com

General Contractor:
Sage Design/Build

Photographer: Edward Caldwell

< The main house glows in the early morning light. The room to the lower left is a greenhouse, with aircraft flaps mounted horizontally to provide summer shade.

Raising the Bar for Ecologically Intelligent Design

"I had a minivan crash through the front of my old house in the Bay Area," says Suzanne Johnson, describing what prompted her move from Northern California's congested Silicon Valley to a sagebrush-strewn slope in the eastern Sierra Nevada Mountains.

Well before that crash, Johnson had been talking with David Arkin and Anni Tilt of Arkin Tilt Architects about remodeling her 1960s ranch house. But life-changing events, including leaving the large high-tech company where she had worked for many years, were driving Johnson to reconsider whether she really wanted to stay in the area.

The minivan incident clinched her decision to buy a five-acre lot on a mountain slope in Gardnerville, Nevada, about a half hour from Lake Tahoe. She had visited the area many times with her parents in the 1970s and often thought it would be a place where she would enjoy living. Johnson selected a lot in a new subdivision, at an elevation of about 5,300 feet, with sweeping views of a broad valley to the east and the rugged peaks of the Sierra Nevadas to the west. Her property sits on the margin between alpine forest and high-desert scrub.

At a corner between the kitchen and dining area, a truth window proves to skeptics that the walls are indeed filled with straw bales.

"The window placement in this home is phenomenal," says Walters. "Every room has a window on at least two walls for natural light." The heights of view windows were fine-tuned in the field. To visitors who comment that the horizontal windows flanking the fireplace in the living area seem a bit low, Walters responds, "Sit on a couch and then tell me. It's perfect." ›

REUSE RECAP

❑ Extensive use of salvaged wood from a dismantled glider hangar, Heinz vinegar vats, and deconstructed buildings in California and Canada

❑ Maple floors in kitchen, entry, powder room and loft reclaimed from a San Francisco school building

❑ Strawbale and PISÉ construction

❑ Flaps from five different types of airplanes to shade the greenhouse

❑ Trellis constructed of salvaged steel posts, railroad tracks and ore cart wheels

❑ Recycled-glass countertops and backsplash

❑ Salvaged steel for woodstove stand, heat shield and decorative uses

❑ Sconces made from used mining screens

❑ Twenty-five percent fly ash content in concrete

❑ Glass for trombe wall bought at salvage yard

❑ Only one tree cut down during construction; reused for trellis post

MORE GREEN STRATEGIES

❑ Design maximizes passive solar heating and cooling, daylighting and views

❑ Energy-efficient building envelope includes structural insulated panel (SIP) roofs, insulated concrete form (ICF) and strawbale walls, and wood-framed walls insulated with recycled cellulose

❑ Five-kilowatt photovoltaic (PV) grid-tied array with battery backup (2.5-kilowatt AstroPower panels on trellis and 2.5-kilowatt Uni-Solar "peel and stick" laminate on standing-seam metal roof)

❑ Solar hot-water collectors for domestic water, space heating and swim-spa

❑ Heat-recovery ventilation system

❑ Trombe wall for passive solar heating of garage

❑ Extensive use of FSC-certified wood

❑ Office furniture made from bamboo plywood

❑ Living roofs on garage and guest house

> *"I think I learned more from the town dump than I learned from school: more about people, more about how life is lived, not elsewhere but here, not in other times but now."*
>
> —Wallace Stegner, "The Town Dump"

Scrapping her plans to remodel her old house, Johnson got back on the phone with Arkin Tilt Architects. "Instead of doing a remodel," she asked, "could you design a new house for me?"

Going All the Way with Ecological Design

Johnson, who had met Arkin a few years earlier at a class he taught on passive solar and ecological design, was keen on working with an architect experienced in designing green homes and keeping toxic materials out of the building process. With the new game plan in place, Arkin Tilt Architects set to work developing design concepts for the site. From the three distinct alternatives they presented to Johnson, she opted for a spirited plan that splits the home into three separate structures. The 2,500-square-foot main house, built on three levels, has an upswept roof form that echoes the soaring mountains. A 350-square-foot guest house and the garage nestle into the hillside; both are topped with living roofs planted with sages and native grasses. A flagstone terrace unites the three buildings.

Now semiretired but still consulting and writing for the high-tech industry, Johnson has long been interested in ecological design and renewable energy, so there was no question that her new house would push the green technology envelope. "I had done solar electric on my old house," she says, "and that hooked me, watching the electric meter run backwards. I really got into it and wanted to go all the way with it."

The buildings employ an impressive range of green design features and construction techniques, from passive and active solar systems to salvaged woods and metals to strawbale walls clad with soil removed during the site excavation.

< Recycled-glass tiles were used for the kitchen backsplash. A custom bar top from Counter Production (counterproduction.com) recycled 150 pounds of manganese glass that Johnson scooped up from the bottom of an old ore cart at a used mining equipment company. In the nineteenth century, manganese was used as an additive to clarify glass, but it fell out of favor because the glass turned the color of amethyst when exposed to sunlight.

Arkin Tilt Architects designed the house to make ❯
the most of views, passive solar heating and
daylighting. "I wanted to be able to sit at a table
in the middle of winter and read the newspaper
without turning any lights on," says Johnson.
The sconces are made from old screens found
at a used mining equipment yard.

Taming the Salvage Beast

On a crisp fall day about six weeks before she is scheduled to move in, I stand with Johnson on a rise a short distance above the house. Sage and dried grasses poke through the snow on the living roofs. Surveying her nearly completed home, which took two years to design and two-and-a-half years to build, she grins and says, "I had no idea how complex it was — no idea!" The plans did call for sophisticated engineering and construction techniques, but in truth some of the complexity also stemmed from Johnson's resolve to use scads of salvage.

The project's construction specifications essentially said, "Use salvaged wood everywhere you can and where you can't, use FSC-certified, sustainably harvested wood," according to Johnson's general contractor, Rick Walters. While Walters focused on tracking down salvaged lumber and metal, Johnson and Arkin Tilt Architects scoured reuse yards for materials such as doors, windows and sinks. The Internet played a vital role in the salvage hunt. When Walters had trouble locating a particular material, he would give Johnson specific keywords and dimensions, and she would search the Internet and post messages to online bulletin boards, leaving Walters's cell number so that people could call him directly with leads on used goods.

A glider hangar in Fremont, California, was the roundabout source for interior siding and exposed beams in the main house and framing lumber in the two sod-roofed buildings. Walters, an accomplished glider pilot, explains: "I was building a clubhouse for a private glider airport up by Pyramid Lake [Nevada], and there were all these old trusses laying on the ground." He

© 2005 Suzanne Johnson

The chimney, shown here, as well as the strawbale walls of the main house, are coated with PISÉ, or pneumatically impacted stabilized earth. Air pressure is used to spray a damp soil mix against formwork or against the wire mesh-wrapped straw bales. The soil all came from Johnson's property. "We excavated 1,000 cubic yards of soil to build the house," Walters explains. "We took some of the soil off-site; the rest we filtered on-site through a screen. We mixed about five parts soil to one part white portland cement" to create the PISÉ mixture.

‹ Trusses from a dismantled glider hangar were used for the ceiling beams in the master bedroom. The ceiling decking is fir from vinegar vats, and the wood for the shelves came from a deconstructed building at the Port of Stockton, California.

learned that when the Fremont glider airport shut down years ago, the hangar was dismantled and the roof trusses donated to the Nevada glider club. The wood trusses languished in the desert sun for ten years.

"I knew they weren't going to use them," Walters says, "because they wouldn't meet the snow load or the wind load in Nevada." Transferring wood, no matter how old it is, from a coastal climate like Fremont's to Nevada's desert can cause shrinkage, warping and other problems, but in this case the timber was already acclimated to Gardnerville's dry climate, so Walters snapped it up. The trusses had never been painted, so lead residue wasn't a concern. "The worst thing," Walters says, "was getting the bird poop off them." His crew wound up using the trusses for ceiling beams in the master bedroom suite, barnwood-style siding in the entry and master bedroom suite, and some framing lumber and trim in the main house and guest house.

Twenty-eight-foot beams supporting the roof above the great room, on the home's second level, were salvaged from a dismantled building in Canada. Maple flooring in the kitchen, bathroom and loft came from an old school in San Francisco. Ceiling decking is fir from a Heinz vinegar factory's soaking vats. "The vinegar smell was noticeable for quite a while," Johnson recalls. "I had some samples in the car with me and the car smelled like vinegar — white vinegar, not balsamic!" she kids.

Kicking the Fossil Fuel Habit

Arkin Tilt Architects designed the main house and guest house for passive solar heating. In winter, concrete floors absorb the warmth of sunlight that streams through south-facing windows. Additional space heating is provided via a high-mass sand bed under the buildings' concrete slabs.

"It's really a pretty simple system," Johnson says. On sunny days, an antifreeze fluid heats up in solar thermal collectors mounted on a south-facing retaining wall below the terrace. A small PV-powered motor circulates the hot fluid through tubes embedded in an insulated sand bed under the buildings' slabs. The sand bed absorbs and stores the heat, gently warming the home.

A backup electric furnace kicks in during spells of cloudy weather (electric equipment and appliances make good sense here because Johnson has five kilowatts of rooftop solar-electric panels). A heat-recovery ventilation system automatically introduces fresh, filtered air at regular intervals, an important consideration for a home built to be as tight and energy efficient as this one.

The house has no air-conditioning. The combination of high thermal mass (from the concrete floors and earthen walls), superior insulation, high-performance windows and passive solar design helps moderate temperatures. In addition, on the colder northeast side of the house, an eighteen-inch duct with a temperature-sensing fan draws nighttime air inside during the summer, helping cool the house.

With its sensitivity to the site conditions and its fluid blending of eco-smart features with beautifully crafted spaces, this home is bound to satisfy the mind, body and spirit. ❖

A south-facing trombe wall warms the unheated garage, protecting the solar-electric system's batteries from freezing. A trombe wall is a low-tech means of collecting and storing heat. Here, a concrete wall with a dark coating is faced with clear glass shingles and copper trim (the glass was purchased at a salvage yard). A small airspace separates the glass from the wall. Heat from the sun passes through the glass, is absorbed by the dark mass wall and transferred to the garage's interior. The pond at the base of the trombe wall is part of a boulder-lined water feature that includes a circulating stream.

‹ A terrace connects the main house, the guest house (left) and the garage (not visible). Solar-electric panels mounted on top of the trellis can be tilted to maximize their exposure to the sun. Solar thermal collectors below the terrace provide hot water and space heating.

Back Story

What Lund's had plenty of was wheels from both ore and fruit carts. The fruit cart wheels, smaller gauge and lighter weight than the ore cart wheels, came off of carts used during fruit harvesting and drying activities in California's Central Valley.

Builder Rick Walters adds, "Once Suzanne had the parts assembled, David and Anni were able to sketch the design. Then we got a welder out here" to put it all together. "We also utilized the steel poles as a ground rod. They're connected to a copper ground rod driven ten feet into the ground, so we're using this whole grid as a lightning arrestor."

The trellis supports a 2.5-kilowatt array of solar-electric panels. They're attached via custom brackets designed by Arkin Tilt Architects that allow the panels to be tilted to maximize their exposure to the sun. "They only need to be adjusted twice a year," Johnson says. "It was optimized for our latitude here." She laughingly refers to the brackets as "Ark'n' Tilts."

"They should patent that name!" Walters jokes.

Reinventing the Wheel:
Where Salvage & Solar Power Meet

For the trellis above Suzanne Johnson's terrace, architect David Arkin envisioned a multipurpose structure that would support the photovoltaic (PV) panels and provide welcome shade. Once the decision was made to use salvaged steel railroad tracks for the trellis's beams, the design details unfolded as the team tracked down additional reclaimed materials.

After salvaged steel poles were found for the vertical supports, Johnson got a call from Arkin's partner, Anni Tilt, who said, "You know, it would be really nice to have some small railroad wheels underneath the railroad track" to connect it to the poles.

Johnson agreed, although her first thought was, "This is going to be interesting!" And in fact, acquiring the wheels wasn't a cakewalk. She journeyed to remote parts of Nevada looking for old steel wheels from ore carts used in mining operations, but they can be hard to find because people collect the carts. "By happenstance," Johnson says, "I was driving through Carson City, saw Lund's Used Mining Equipment, stopped in, and she said, 'Oh yeah, I've got plenty of those.'"

Ore cart and fruit cart wheels › support the railroad-track trellis. This post is fashioned from the single tree that had to be removed from the site during construction. Other posts are salvaged steel.

Back Story

Winging It: Inventive Responses to a Tough Climate

Standing with Suzanne Johnson and builder Rick Walters outside the greenhouse that encloses Johnson's swim-spa (a small exercise pool that creates a current to swim against), I admire the silvery fins mounted on the greenhouse exterior. "That started as a joke," Johnson admits.

One day, Johnson explains, she and her architect, David Arkin, "were looking at the salvage places for something to use as shading fins, and as a joke I said, 'Maybe through Rick we could get glider wings.'" Walters happens to be a champion glider pilot who moved to the Eastern Sierra to take advantage of the extraordinary soaring conditions. "We asked Rick but he said no, that glider wings are pretty flimsy," Johnson says.

"They're made of fiberglass, and they won't hold up in the sun," Walters points out.

"So then we went to airplane parts," Johnson continues. "Rick thought there weren't going to be many around and they were going to be way too expensive."

"I took Suzanne and David down to the airport, to a wrecking yard," Walters recalls. "We were just poking around, and the next thing I know, it was on the plans."

Johnson says, grinning, "That was sort of where we learned you don't kid about things with David!"

Walters mounted the forty-five aluminum aircraft flaps on the greenhouse exterior with custom brackets designed to withstand winds that howl down from the mountains. "The flaps are from five different airplane types, but the majority are from the Piper Cherokee," Walters says, "the most common airplane ever built. It's got a twelve-inch chord and it worked out perfectly for the shading."

Walters shows me one of the Piper flaps, an elongated section that's normally hinged to an airplane wing to increase lift or drag. "It's eighty-five inches long. An airworthy one is worth $400 dollars, but one in this condition — it's a little dinged — is worth $40. I bent some of them back into shape or cut them, and I had them sandblasted. We didn't want a shiny aluminum part reflecting sun."

^
A wrecking yard was the source for aircraft flaps > that now shade Suzanne Johnson's greenhouse. Photos © 2005 Arkin Tilt Architects.

Discarded billboards that once advertised PT Cruisers and Levi's jeans were cut into strips and layered on the exterior walls, shown here before installation of the final layer of translucent polycarbonate sheathing.

Putting It Back Together

Where: Minneapolis, Minnesota

Architect & Builder:
LOCUS Architecture
612.706.5600
locusarchitecture.com

Photographers:
John Christenson, Robert Meier

Deconstructing a '50s Rambler and Reconstructing a Bold New Home

A new house is turning heads in the Lakes area southwest of downtown Minneapolis, in an architecturally diverse neighborhood of 1920s Tudors, mid-century ramblers and more contemporary homes. Wynne Yelland, a principal in the firm LOCUS Architecture, says that "One very strong reaction from the neighborhood has been, 'Why do you have a car on the front of the house?'"

Why indeed? From behind the home's outermost skin of translucent polycarbonate panels, colorful graphics from salvaged billboards beckon. Yelland and Paul Neseth, partners at LOCUS Architecture, a Minneapolis design/build firm, layered the structure with strips of vinyl billboards that once advertised PT Cruisers and Levi's jeans.

‹ At night the billboard graphics fade. At the back of the house, the kitchen and the master bedroom above it bump out so that their walls nearly touch the polycarbonate skin. Above the back porch and at the right corner, the polycarbonate is held off from the building by about three and a half feet, creating spaces sheltered from the weather. Recessed lights in the soffit give these spaces a lantern-like glow.

Low-maintenance materials play off each other, including a steel roof and three types of siding: fiber-cement, polycarbonate and corrugated steel on the dormer. The façade's appearance changes depending on light conditions, with the billboard graphics most prominent when skies are overcast.

REUSE RECAP

- ❏ Existing one-story house deconstructed down to foundation
- ❏ Most of disassembled materials reused, including framing lumber, roof sheathing and plumbing fixtures
- ❏ Salvaged vinyl billboards used as building paper
- ❏ Salvaged slate chalkboard used for wall finish
- ❏ Reclaimed maple and oak flooring

MORE GREEN STRATEGIES

- ❏ Urban location within walking distance of retail district, parks and lakes
- ❏ Energy-efficient design
- ❏ Unique wall construction designed to protect structure from moisture infiltration
- ❏ Durable, low-maintenance materials inside and out
- ❏ Extensive use of FSC-certified wood

> The far wall of the dining room is reclaimed slate chalkboard from a local salvage yard. The countertops at left and center are concrete. Wall panels are medium-density fiberboard with a birch veneer that cleans up easily and won't require painting. "We tried to use things that are going to last longer than the typical ten- to fifteen-year remodeling horizon," says Yelland. "The concrete floors could last 200 years. We used a lot of steel, which can be recycled and is also very durable. The plywood walls will take a beating, and they're going to look good even with some distress, whereas drywall tends to look bad on day two."

Litter that Lasts Forever

Neseth and Yelland, who designed and built this two-and-half-story house on spec, reused more than 600 square feet of salvaged vinyl from three billboards that originally measured fourteen-by-forty-eight feet. In addition to making an aesthetic and environmental statement, the billboards protect the house from moisture infiltration.

"We didn't just cut strips," Neseth points out. "We did it to obscure the images to a certain degree so that they're not legible on the outside. And we did it in such a way that we were in control of the graphics, so we weren't just taking something found and applying it. We wanted to manipulate it so that it worked for us, and not have such a strong product reference."

Billboard advertising is by nature ephemeral, replaced after a short time by in-your-face images of the next new thing. But vinyl — the material that most billboards are printed on — is engineered to last. "Litter on a stick" aptly reflects how some people feel about the larger-than-life advertisements that pepper our highways and streetscapes.*

With no infrastructure in place to recycle vinyl trash, disposal is a mounting issue. "One of Paul's big theories from the very beginning of our practice," Yelland says, "was trying to link the burden of things with the benefit of things. So if there's a benefit to a material, where is it coming from and who has to live next to wherever they're making it or where they're digging it out of the ground? That led the two of us to start trying to also minimize the burden of the landfill."

< On the second floor, the catwalk leads to the master bedroom and another bedroom. The steel staircase continues up to the third floor, where there are two more bedrooms.

* If the expression "litter on a stick" resonates with you, check out Dolores Hayden's book, **A Field Guide to Sprawl.** With eye-popping aerial photographs and zippy definitions of land-use terms from ball pork to snout house to zoomburb, Hayden decodes how unchecked development is damaging the American landscape.

© 2005 John Christenson

^
The wood flooring in the original house wasn't salvageable, so the architects used maple and oak flooring reclaimed from other buildings.

Just Say No to Bulldozers

The reused billboard wrap symbolizes the firm's commitment to exploring sustainable building strategies, but behind the scenes, Neseth and Yelland employed other less flashy waste-reduction strategies. The original house on the property, a 900-square-foot, single-story rambler built in 1952, didn't have much to recommend it besides its appealing location.

Other developers might have called in a bulldozer, but the LOCUS team took a different tack: they *deconstructed* the building board by board rather than demolishing it. "Without saving every two-foot section of two-by-four, we took everything we could have out of that place, and it went back in," Neseth says. The original framing lumber, roof sheathing, plumbing fixtures and other salvaged components went back into the building of the new house. Certain materials that are nearly impossible to reuse or recycle, such as painted drywall or asphalt shingles, did end up in the dump. (See page 126 for more about deconstruction.)

The reconstructed house — 2,400 square feet of living space on two-and-a-half floors, and a 600-square-foot finished basement — sits on the original foundation. By expanding the building upward rather than outward, LOCUS barely extended the original footprint. In addition to reusing materials from the deconstructed building, they focused on creating a house that's energy efficient, low maintenance and durable.

The home's exterior wall system was designed to be highly resistant to moisture, a critical sustainability consideration since damage from mold and other moisture-related problems is the main reason buildings fail. There is no insulation in the wall cavities; instead, exterior walls have a continuous layer of rigid insulation outside the framing layer, along with a continuous vapor barrier outside the wall sheathing on the first floor and much of the second floor. Building paper and the billboards were applied on the outside of the insulation. Between the billboards and the outermost skin of translucent polycarbonate, a one-and-a-half-inch airspace allows the building to shed any trapped moisture.

Neseth is quick to point out that sustainability extends beyond basic green design tenets such as energy efficiency, health and durability: "A purely sustainable thing is something that is as aesthetically appealing as possible and as progressive as possible. It has to be a great place to live. And in our case, that means not only being good for the soul but also challenging you a little bit. It ought to make you think a bit about our place in the world." ❖

In the double-height living room, large windows in the ❯ southwest corner admit daylight and warmth. Most of the framing lumber from the original house was reused. In addition, about 80 percent of the new dimensional lumber and plywood used for framing was FSC certified. The FSC wood was cost competitive with non-certified wood, but Neseth notes that "we had to do a little more planning to get it."

Inside Scoop

Courtesy of The Reuse People

Deconstruct, Don't Demolish

Bulldozing a house and burying the shattered structure in a hole in the ground sounds perverse, yet it happens every day in neighborhoods across the country. An alternative is *deconstruction*, which simply means systematically dismantling a building and salvaging its parts for reuse.

To be sure, deconstruction's been around as long as . . . well, as long as construction has. Over the last few decades, however, high labor costs and increased mechanization have made it faster and cheaper to crunch an unwanted structure than manually un-build it. But with landfill tipping fees, the cost of new lumber, and environmental consciousness all on the upswing, deconstruction is gaining ground.

Tax Deduction for Deconstruction

In Alameda, California, on the site of a former naval air station across the bay from San Francisco, Ted Reiff runs The Reuse People, a nonprofit organization that salvages building materials and sells them for reuse (thereusepeople.org). Over the years they've deconstructed dozens of structures across California, from decommissioned military bases to Hollywood sets to moguls' mansions to seen-better-days bungalows. Roofing tiles, framing lumber, fireplace mantels, kitchen cabinets, you name it — if it's reusable, it gets trucked back to The Reuse People store for resale to the public.

"The alternative to deconstruction is to have the building demo-ed," says Reiff. "The materials would then go to MRFs," pronounced murfs, an acronym for the material recovery facilities whose business is to keep recyclable waste out of landfills. "But that's recycling — it means lower value and higher energy costs because the material's got to be ground up, chipped up, remanufactured. With deconstruction, we're using a cabinet as a cabinet, a door as a door. That's the key for us — it's truly reuse."

Deconstruction usually costs more than demolition. So why bother? If the environmental benefits alone don't sway you, consider this: many deconstruction outfits are 501 (c)(3) nonprofits, which means building owners can often claim a sizeable deduction on their tax returns for the donation value of the reusable materials pulled from the building. In many cases, the tax savings offset the added cost of deconstruction. (Be sure to consult a tax professional for advice.)

Deconstruction is also typically gentler on the site than bulldozing, a real plus if you're concerned about protecting landscaping or soil quality on your property.

"The biggest disadvantage to deconstruction is time," Reiff cautions. "If it takes an excavator a day, it'll take us ten." He urges homeowners and general contractors to plan well in advance for deconstruction, because waiting until the last minute may leave you staring into the bulldozer's maw.*

---

* Looking for a decon crew? Don't expect to find a listing for "deconstruction" in the Yellow Pages. Call your local salvage yard or building materials reuse store for recommendations (look under "Salvage Merchandise" or "Building Materials–Used"). Or get a copy of the **Directory of Wood-Framed Building Deconstruction and Reused Building Materials Companies** from the USDA's Forest Products Laboratory (treesearch.fs.fed.us). On the Internet, deconstructioninstitute.com is chock-a-block full of handy info about the deconstruction process.

Side Effects

The Vinyl Debate

Vinyl. It's everywhere. According to The Vinyl Institute, a trade association representing the vinyl manufacturing industry, it's "the second largest volume plastic produced in the world," with 14.6 billion pounds of vinyl resin produced in North America in 2000 alone (vinylinstitute.org). First developed in the 1920s, this inexpensive, versatile material — also known as polyvinyl chloride, or PVC — turns up in a mind-boggling array of products in our homes, from exterior siding to window frames, from piping to electrical conduits, from shower curtains to kids' toys.

So what's the problem? For the past decade there's been heated debate about the environmental and health impacts of vinyl manufacturing, use and disposal. While the vinyl industry stands behind the safety of its products, the environmental group, Greenpeace, calls vinyl "the poison plastic," noting that "the production of PVC creates and releases one of the most toxic chemicals — dioxin" (greenpeace.org). The Healthy Building Network, a project of the Washington, D.C.–based Institute for Self-Reliance, calls PVC "the worst plastic from an environmental health perspective, posing major hazards in its manufacture, product life and disposal" (healthybuilding.net/pvc).

Humor, Horror and the Helfands' Vinyl Siding

In 2002, documentary filmmakers Judith Helfand and Daniel B. Gold debuted their film *Blue Vinyl,* subtitled "A Toxic Odyssey for the Whole Family." It's a highly entertaining and provocative look at the polyvinyl chloride industry and Ms. Helfand's attempts to find a healthier replacement for the blue vinyl siding on her parents' Long Island, New York, home. The film presents her quest with equal doses of humor and horror, and ultimately poses the question, "Is it possible to make products that never hurt anyone at any point in their life cycle — when manufactured, when used, or when disposed of?" (Find out more about the film at bluevinyl.org; check out the associated consumer education and advocacy group at myhouseisyourhouse.org.)

Architects Paul Neseth and Wynne Yelland, who gave salvaged vinyl billboards new life as building paper in the house shown in the previous pages, acknowledge the complexity of sustainable building design. Talking with Yelland in his firm's San Francisco office (Neseth and Yelland are based in Minneapolis; their partner Steven Rajninger runs their West Coast operation), I ask about the upsides and downsides of reusing vinyl billboards.

"I don't know what the right answer is," he admits. "Once the stuff's out there, should we be finding a use for it and making a back-end industry for this thing? Or should we be saying, 'Nobody should be using this,' so they stop manufacturing it? If Paul and I came down on one side or the other, we'd say we ought to reuse it and at the same time put pressure on people not to be making stuff like this."

Neseth agrees: "The short-term solution is to reuse" discarded vinyl, but "the long-term solution is to not produce it in the first place."

The Vinyl Stops Here

Where do I stand on this one? If you've got vinyl siding on your house, I don't suggest you rip it off, like Helfand did at her parents' house — because then what are you going to do with all that virtually indestructible stuff? But in my own home-improvement projects, I've decided to err on the side of caution, and until we have more definitive answers about vinyl's safety, I try to seek out PVC-free alternatives.

Filmmakers Judith Helfand and Daniel B. Gold at the intersection ❯ of Trust Drive and Corporate Boulevard in Baton Rouge, Louisiana. Much of North America's PVC is produced in Louisiana.

Back to Basics

Where: Healdsburg, California

Architect: Siegel & Strain Architects
Emeryville, California
510.547.8092
siegelstrain.com

General Contractor:
Talia Developments

Photographer: J. D. Peterson
Photography

A Strawbale Dogtrot in Sonoma's Wine Country

In mid-November I drive through Sonoma County's Dry Creek Valley, just north of Healdsburg, California, on my way to Henry Siegel's weekend home. This time of year the wine-tasting crowds have dwindled and now that I'm off the freeway, traffic is light. As I wind my way on country roads past vineyards where the leaves have turned a brilliant yellow, hawks circle above in the late-afternoon sunshine. I'm only an hour and a half from San Francisco but already I feel the stresses of city life melting away.

The road grows increasingly narrow until I'm on a steep gravel drive that makes a hairpin turn up to Siegel's two-and-a-half acre property. I leave my car in a pullout well below the house and climb a terraced walkway through a meadow of tall fluttering grasses. It had rained a few days earlier, marking the end of Northern California's six-month dry season, and a loamy scent rises from the earth.

The house is barely two years old but already it feels at one with the land, settled in amid towering Douglas firs, moss-covered oaks and mature California bay laurels. Siegel, a founding principal of Siegel & Strain Architects,* and his wife, Kyra, built

‹ Door and window frames are lustrous mahogany certified by the FSC to have been sustainably harvested.

* Siegel & Strain Architects, a leader in environmentally sustainable design, has won awards for projects ranging from San Francisco's Jackson Brewery, a historic building converted into a mixed-use project with live/work condos and a restaurant, to Camp Arroyo, an environmental education camp for children. Check out their work at siegelstrain.com.

A loft accessible from the dogtrot provides play space for the couple's children. The dogtrot's walls are finished with an FSC-certified maple plywood; some interior walls and the ceilings are finished with a birch plywood that has an FSC-certified, medium-density fiberboard (MDF) core.

Siegal considered, and ultimately dropped, > plans for glass barn-door sliders to close off the dogtrot. "We just haven't needed them," he says. "It's not that big a deal to walk across the breezeway at night, even in the winter."

REUSE RECAP

- Strawbale construction
- Thirty-five percent fly ash in concrete
- Recycled-glass countertop in bathroom
- Recycled cellulose above ceiling

MORE GREEN FEATURES

- Small size of home minimizes site disturbance and conserves resources and energy
- Sheltered outdoor room extends living space for much of the year
- Designed to be comfortable without air-conditioning despite high summer temperatures
- FSC-certified products include framing lumber, mahogany door and window frames, MDF cores of birch plywood, and maple plywood ("apply ply")
- Energy Star appliances and a very low-energy ConServ refrigerator
- High-efficiency water heater for household use and radiant-floor heating
- Durable, low-maintenance materials including fiber-cement siding, metal roof, and concrete floors and counters

the house as a place where they and their children could take a break from the daily hubbub back home in Berkeley, across the bay from San Francisco.

Celebrating the Good Life

In many ways this is the archetypical vacation cottage: a sheltered site with bucolic views, casual rooms designed to bring people together, an easy flow between indoors and out, few extraneous flourishes to distract from the business of relaxing. That it's built with recycled and other eco-friendly materials almost seems beside the point. Strawbale walls, sustainably harvested woods, smart design that eliminates the need for air-conditioning — these all play a supporting role to the home's low-key design that quietly celebrates the good life.

The walkway leads to the center of the home, an open-air dogtrot where, fittingly, the family dog Shadow waits to greet me, black tail wagging. Siegel based the home's design on the humble dogtrot-style dwelling common in the rural South before the days of air-conditioning. It's essentially two small cottages linked by a breezeway, with a metal-clad gable roof spanning the entire structure. The breezeway, or dogtrot, is open on two sides and serves as a sheltered outdoor room.

"We spend a lot of time out here," Siegel says as we stand in the dogtrot. The house is "only about 1,200 square feet, but it feels commodious. In some ways it feels just as comfortable as our Craftsman house in Berkeley, which is twice as big. It's partly because we spend a lot of

< Shared views through the spaces and high
  ceilings make the small house feel spacious.

Side Effects

Waiter – There's Fly Ash in My Concrete!

Fly ash, a waste by-product of coal-burning power plants, is the fine residue removed from the flue gas by the plant's pollution control devices. Traditionally fly ash has been dumped in landfills, but there are better alternatives, including adding it to concrete.

The primary ingredients of concrete are portland cement, aggregates like sand and gravel, and water. Portland cement manufacturing is energy intensive, producing significant carbon dioxide (CO_2) emissions that contribute to global warming. Substituting recycled fly ash for some of the portland cement in concrete reduces CO_2 emissions to the atmosphere. According to the American Coal Ash Association, each ton of fly ash used in concrete reduces CO_2 emissions by approximately one ton, the equivalent of about two months of CO_2 emissions from a car. In the United States alone, CO_2 emissions are reduced by more than

time using the outdoor room."

The structure on the south side of the dogtrot is the main living and dining area, a high-ceilinged room that's about thirty feet long and fourteen feet wide. On the other side of the dogtrot, a twenty-two-foot-long by fourteen-foot-wide space houses a bedroom, bathroom, and storage and utility areas. Concrete floors, stained a golden hue inside the home and left a natural gray in the dogtrot, contain 35 percent recycled fly ash. (For more about fly ash, see Side Effects, left.) Tubes embedded in the slab circulate hot water to provide gentle radiant space heating; radiant heat warms surfaces and people rather than air, so it can be an energy-efficient way to heat rooms with high ceilings.

Hay Is for Horses, Straw Is for Houses

At Siegel's residence, the reuse story lies behind the walls, where straw bales are stacked like giant bricks within the post-and-beam framing. Building with straw bales gets high green marks, in part because it's an abundant, recycled and rapidly renewable resource. Unlike hay, which is grown specifically for fodder, straw is the waste that's left over after harvesting rice, wheat, barley and other grains. Straw bales do an outstanding job of insulating, helping keep the house cool in summer and cozy in winter.

One weekend when the house was under construction, the couple invited over friends and colleagues to help heave the seventy-five-pound bales into place. "It's the modern-day equivalent of a barn raising," Siegel says. "It was really fun."

"People loved it," Kyra recalls, smiling as she tells about a friend who helped that day. Now whenever he comes to visit, he points to one particular wall, joking, "That's my wall!"

Heavy mesh attached to the outside of the stacked bales provides lateral strength (this is seismically active country, after all), as does the stucco that coats the interior and exterior walls. Some builders go out of their way to accentuate the rounded edges and sculptural shapes that strawbale construction makes possible, but Siegel went for a crisper look with straighter lines and squared edges. For the exterior, he chose a gray-on-gray color scheme that he calls "anti-Tuscan," a relief from the region's obsession with shades of ochre.

Old-Fashioned Cool

With dense tree coverage and ridges to the west and south, the site was never a candidate for either passive solar design or photovoltaics. "The whole strategy," says Siegel, "was if we can't get passive solar heating and we can't generate our energy, let's just eliminate the biggest user of energy, which is cooling."

Summer days here can be beastly hot, with temperatures in the hundreds not uncommon, so the highly insulating strawbale walls are part of a well-considered strategy to keep the home cool without relying on air-conditioning. Other features that hold down energy use while keeping the home comfortable include recycled cellulose insulation (made from

thirteen million tons per year thanks to the use of fly ash in concrete.

Besides the environmental benefits of avoided landfill disposal and reduced CO_2 emissions, adding fly ash can improve the concrete's quality by reducing permeability and increasing strength and durability. While some construction specifications limit fly ash content to 15 or 20 percent of the portland cement content, many experienced engineers and contractors are using mixes with as much as 30 to 50 percent fly ash with superior results.

A high volume of fly ash may slow the concrete's curing time, so if you plan to use it, work with a contractor or supplier who is familiar with its properties. Fly ash concrete is typically priced the same as ordinary concrete without fly ash.

Learn more about fly ash from the American Coal Ash Association (acca-usa.org). The City of Austin's Green Building Program has good fact sheets about fly ash and many other green building topics at ci.austin.tx.us/greenbuilder.

Two bays on either side of the main living area are clad with fiber-cement boards, a durable, low-maintenance siding material.

old newspapers) above the ceiling; deep eaves shading the double-pane, low-e-squared windows (a low-e-squared coating on glass reduces winter heat loss through the windows as well as reducing direct solar heat gain); and thermal mass from the concrete floors and stucco walls to moderate temperature swings.

"The basic rule for this house," Siegel says, "is what people always used to do before air-conditioning, which is open the windows at night and close them in the morning as soon as it gets warmer outside than inside. And then as soon as it gets cooler outside than inside, you open them up again."

The open-air dogtrot as well as the narrowness of the whole structure promote cross ventilation. Siegel admits that on hot days, "it starts to get slightly uncomfortable in the late afternoon, so you turn on the ceiling fans. That's enough to keep it comfortable through pretty much the hottest weather."

One warm evening last summer, high tech met small town when the multipurpose dogtrot transformed into a home theater. Siegel had borrowed his office's digital projector and after dark plugged his laptop into it and popped in a DVD. "We hung a sheet up in the dogtrot," he says, "and watched a movie sitting outside at night. It was fabulous, like a mini drive-in theater." ❖

Courtesy of Siegel & Strain Architects

Side Effects

A Home for Ag-Waste

Straw bales may never catch on as a mainstream building material, but they make good sense for some custom-built homes, especially those in relatively dry climates and close to agricultural areas where straw is abundant. A renewable resource, straw is waste fiber left over after harvesting rice, wheat, barley and other grains. Using building products made from straw and other agricultural waste fiber puts unwanted material to good use, and in some cases may even help reduce pressure to harvest our forests.

Larry Strain (right), Henry Siegel's partner at Siegel & Strain Architects, uses a chain saw to trim a bale to the right size at Siegel's bale-raising gathering. Extra hands are much appreciated when it comes time to stack the bales within the post-and-beam frame. Dimensions vary, but a typical bale weighs seventy to eighty pounds and measures approximately forty-six inches long by twenty-three inches wide by fifteen inches high.

Even if a strawbale house isn't in your future, you can still use ag-waste for many home-improvement projects. Here are just a few of the recycled ag-waste products available today:

❏ Dow BioProducts, a division of the giant Dow Chemical Company, makes a panel product called *Woodstalk.* An alternative to particleboard and medium-density fiberboard, Woodstalk is wheat straw bound with a polyurethane resin instead of the urea formaldehyde resin used in many composite wood products. (Urea formaldehyde is a respiratory irritant and carcinogen, so it's a good idea to avoid building products and furnishings that might offgas it into your home.) Woodstalk can be used for cabinets, millwork, furniture, shelves, flooring underlayment and more. Check it out at dow.com/bioprod.

❏ *Neil Kelly Cabinets* in Portland, Oregon, uses melamine-laminated wheatboard as the standard interior for their cabinet cases. Wheatboard is a generic term for panel products made from wheat straw. Neil Kelly uses water-based finishes, natural oils and low-VOC paints on their products (for more about VOCs, see page 60). Options for their cabinet exteriors include bamboo, FSC-certified woods such as maple, cherry, red oak, pine, alder and red birch, and reclaimed woods. Find out more at neilkellycabinets.com.

❏ Environ Biocomposites in Mankato, Minnesota, manufactures panel products from agricultural waste and rapidly renewable resources. Their *Dakota Burl,* a unique panel made mostly from sunflower seed hulls, can be used for tables, wall paneling, furniture, cabinets and other interior applications. The company also makes *Environ,* a board product made with recycled paper, soy flour and pigment, and *Biofiber,* a wheat-straw panel. Go to environbiocomposites.com.

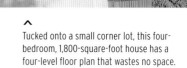

^
Tucked onto a small corner lot, this four-bedroom, 1,800-square-foot house has a four-level floor plan that wastes no space.

Principles into Practice

Where: Belmont, California

Architect: Arkin Tilt Architects
Berkeley, California
510.528.9830
arkintilt.com

Builder: Ebcon Development

Photographer: Edward Caldwell

Arkin Tilt Architects at Work, and a Family at Home

On a sunny Saturday, dozens of strangers traipse through Gladwyn d'Souza and Martina de la Torre's house in Belmont, a city of 26,000 people about halfway between San Francisco and San Jose. The couple, along with their son and daughter, moved into their newly built house several months earlier. On this day they have opened their doors to the community as part of a Solar Homes Tour organized to give people an up-close look at photovoltaic and solar hot-water systems.*

Throughout the day, d'Souza and de la Torre, along with their architect, David Arkin, and two solar installation experts, answer a barrage of questions from visitors who seem as curious about the home's green features as they are about its renewable energy systems. The tour-goers exclaim over the intricate plumbing of the combined solar hot-water/space-heating system, check out the storage capacity of the energy-efficient refrigerator, and snap photos of bamboo flooring, recycled-glass counters and exposed beams of reclaimed wood.

I ask d'Souza what put him on the path to building a green home, and he explains that in addition to environmental concerns, an important motivation was that their daughter has asthma, so they wanted to create a healthier home free of allergens and mold.

< At the center of the home, the stairwell tower lets in light and draws out warm air, helping cool the home naturally.

* Solar power isn't just for back-to-the-landers. Growing numbers of city dwellers and suburbanites are harvesting the sun's power for electricity, hot water and space heating. To see for yourself how well today's systems work, head out on a Solar Homes Tour. Sponsored by the American Solar Energy Society, the tours take place every October across the United States. Find out more at ases.org.

The stair tower, framed with reclaimed Douglas fir floor joists, doubles as a library. On the left, a salvaged door hung on a barn-door track also does double duty: it's the door to the master bedroom suite and serves as a ladder for reaching the upper bookshelves. Transoms above the door promote natural ventilation and brighten interior spaces with daylight.

Solar-electric panels do double duty as an ❯ awning over the front door. Sliding screens made from sustainably harvested Spanish cedar provide privacy while letting in dappled sunlight during the day.

REUSE RECAP

- ❏ Wall and bookshelf framing from reclaimed Douglas fir floor joists
- ❏ Trusses made from salvaged beams
- ❏ Ceiling decking from vinegar-barrel staves
- ❏ Exterior soffit material from salvaged siding
- ❏ Salvaged doors, including garage doors reclaimed from a dismantled elementary school
- ❏ Roofing shingles made from recycled rubber and plastic
- ❏ Kitchen bar top from recycled glass

MORE GREEN FEATURES

- ❏ Relatively small size of house to reduce energy and resource use
- ❏ Urban infill site, within walking distance to public transit and retail services
- ❏ Structure configured to preserve two large coast live oaks on property
- ❏ 2.5-kilowatt photovoltaic system (on roof and awning above front door) sized to meet 100 percent of home's electricity needs
- ❏ Rooftop solar thermal collectors provide most of the heat for household water and space heating
- ❏ Passive solar design, including south-facing windows and thermal-mass walls and floors, moderates indoor temperatures year-round
- ❏ Stair tower allows heat to rise and flow out, cooling the home without air-conditioning, and introduces daylight into the home's core
- ❏ Energy-efficient fluorescent lighting and Energy Star appliances
- ❏ Framing lumber is FSC certified, as is redwood cribbing on balconies
- ❏ Custom sliding doors and screen panels from sustainably harvested Spanish cedar
- ❏ Bamboo flooring

In 1999, the couple purchased a 4,900-square-foot corner lot with good southern exposure, located within walking distance of Belmont's compact downtown and a commuter rail station. "We picked a city infill location," d'Souza says, in part because it allows for "a healthier, walking-intensive lifestyle." They selected Arkin Tilt Architects to design a home that would be as environmentally responsible as it is family-friendly.

At just over 1,800 square feet, the house isn't large by today's new-home standards. But high ceilings, copious daylight, shared views through rooms and a clever multilevel floor plan give the four-bedroom house an expansive feel. On weekends, the children's grandmother lives with the family; recognizing that her physical abilities may change as time goes on, the entire main level of the home, including the guest room and bath, was designed to be wheelchair accessible from the street.

Health and environmental considerations drove decisions about equipment, systems, ventilation design and materials. The home has radiant-floor heating supplied largely by solar collectors on the roof — essentially free energy from the sun. For people with respiratory problems, radiant heat can be a better option than a forced-air furnace because it doesn't blow burnt dust or other irritants around the house.* Smooth surface flooring — including concrete in the main living areas and bamboo in the bedrooms — is easier to keep free of dust and other pollutants than carpet. And d'Souza was drawn to building with reclaimed solid wood in part because he thought it might be healthier than the alternative: using newly manufactured products that might offgas chemicals for years to come.

Throughout the day, sunlight dances across the warm hues of the salvaged wood, much as it plays against two mature oak trees whose sprawling limbs shelter the home's west side. Arkin Tilt Architects designed the building's shape and footprint to preserve these grand old trees, real community treasures in this densely developed neighborhood.

< The ceiling decking is made from old vinegar-barrel staves. Roof trusses are made from salvaged beams. "The wood that was being harvested a hundred years ago was better than the wood that's being harvested today," says architect David Arkin. "So not only are we not cutting down trees by using reclaimed wood, we're using better materials."

* Breathe easier. Go to the American Lung Association's Web site, healthhouse.org, for tips on maintaining good indoor air quality in your home.

Fold-down desks in the study and play area make >
efficient use of space. The top shelves are backed
with clear glazing to share light between the bathroom and study area. Bedroom floors are bamboo.

A well-considered daylighting design animates the
home with ever-changing sparkles of light. The
fourth-floor stair landing, which leads to a roof
terrace, has a glass floor and an interior window
for letting daylight into the heart of the home.

In the great room, the exposed roof trusses are made from salvaged Douglas fir beams, and the ceiling decking is fashioned from old barrel staves taken from nine-foot-diameter Heinz vinegar barrels. A daylight-filled stair tower at the home's core has walls built from remilled Douglas fir floor joists. This deep wall framing doubles as shelves to accommodate the family's many books. Between the kitchen and dining area, a recycled-glass bar top sparkles in the sunshine.

New Contexts for Old Stuff

The process for sourcing salvaged materials varies from project to project, depending on the homeowner's inclinations, experience and budget. For the d'Souza/de la Torre residence, Arkin Tilt Architects took the lead on tracking down the salvaged materials. They relied on a number of sources, with the majority of the large timbers and the vinegar-barrel staves coming from Recycled Lumberworks in Ukiah, north of San Francisco (oldwoodguy.com).

Sourcing salvaged materials clearly takes more work than specifying brand-new materials, so over lunch one day in a sunny café near their office, I ask David Arkin and Anni Tilt why they do it.

"We come at it from two angles," Arkin says. "Landfills are filling with construction and demolition waste that could be reused, so certainly trying to be friendlier to the earth is one whole side. But the other side is the history and character and, in some instances, higher quality that comes with salvaged materials."

Arkin's interest in salvaged building materials crystallized in the mid-1990s, when he was the project architect for the design and construction of the Solar

Concrete floors provide thermal mass for passive solar heating and the radiant-floor heating system. Stair treads are Douglas fir harvested by an urban forestry operation.

Living Center in Hopland, California. The curving one-story structure, built with rice-straw bales, is a demonstration center for solar and green building technologies.* During the design process, Jeff Oldham, the Center's project manager at the time, came across hundreds of toilet tank lids piled up at a local salvage yard. "He wanted to know if we could use them to tile the Center's bathroom floors," Arkin remembers. "I said 'No, I think they'll be too slippery, but we could probably use them on the walls because the code requires a wainscot up to four feet in public bathrooms.'"

The ceramic toilet tank–lid wainscot went up with great success, along with bathroom-stall partitions built of colorful recycled plastic and countless other recycled, reclaimed and eco-friendly materials. "It was a solution that was better than any other we could have come up with," Arkin recalls, "and it was because of the desire to use salvaged and recycled materials. For me, that illustrates why we do this."

Anni Tilt, Arkin's design partner and wife, points to an even earlier influence. "I've always been a scrounger," she says, laughing. "As my cousin put it, we have a thrifty grandmother and it seems to be in our blood. She would take Christmas cards from friends and cut them up for gift tags, old jars were transformed into vases with a little paint, and on and on. But in the past, working for other firms, it was all I could do to get salvaged wood in a project. Generally so much of a project is thought out beforehand — it's a completely conceived idea; the process is set up so that everything is manufactured and specified."

Working with salvage does require flexibility during design and construction, however. "You can't have a rigid concept from the get-go

* The Solar Living Center, a twelve-acre demonstration site for renewable energy and sustainable living technologies, is the headquarters of the educational nonprofit organization Solar Living Institute (solarliving.org). The Center is owned by Gaiam Real Goods, a leading retailer of renewable energy systems and other products for green living (realgoods.com).

unless you actually have pieces you're working with," says Tilt.

Arkin adds, "I enjoy the bit of architectural jujitsu that happens when you're working with salvaged materials. You never quite know what it is you're going to find, but you know the right piece when you find it so you sometimes have to make adjustments in other parts of the design."

Love, Labor and Building with Junk

Arkin is quick to dispel the notion that building with old stuff will save money. "Often there is some economy in getting a used thing as opposed to a new thing, but there is often extra effort that goes into the handling of it. An old door may cost $20 or $30 but if you have to have the carpenter build the jamb that would otherwise have come prehung with a new door, it could easily add up to what a new door would cost."

Tilt agrees, noting that it's important to "separate the labor from the material costs. If you're having a contractor do it, you're talking about labor costs. But if you're doing it yourself, then maybe you don't care if you spend a weekend stripping a door. Then it's a labor of love."

DIY projects aside, good communication among homeowner, architect and contractor are critical when building with old stuff. Arkin emphasizes that the relationship among all parties needs to be "based in trust. Nobody likes surprises, so if we're starting something and it looks like it's going to cost more than the standard thing, then we have a conversation about it ahead of time. You weigh the costs and benefits. That's true for everything." ❖

Garage doors were salvaged from an old school in Berkeley, California. Over the years, school maintenance staff replaced broken panes with different types of glass, giving the doors a one-of-a-kind appeal.

Inside Scoop

From Old Tires to New Roofs: Recycled Shingles and Shakes

Rich-grained old timbers, sparkling recycled glass and distinctive salvaged doors can add a dash of character to any new home. More prosaic materials like recycled roofing shingles also do a good turn for the environment by putting waste to good use. Several companies now offer roofing materials designed to look like slate shingles or cedar shakes but are made from blends of recycled industrial plastics, automobile-tire rubber and other additives. These products are relatively new, so long-term durability isn't proven but some manufacturers offer forty- or fifty-year warranties, with pricing comparable to wood shingles and much less than natural stone.

Products include Majestic Slate from EcoStar (premiumroofs.com), Enviroshake from Wellington Polymer Technology (enviroshake.com), Euroslate from GEM (euroslate.ca) and Authentic Roof 2000 from Crowe Building Products (authentic-roof.com).

Side Effects

Maximum Kick with Minimum Impact

David Arkin and Anni Tilt's approach to architecture puts equal weight on outstanding design and environmental responsibility. Some people call that sustainable design; Arkin and Tilt call it "Maximum Kick with Minimum Impact." Here are five goals that form the foundation of their practice.

Harmonize with the Site
The site is the starting point. We assess the site conditions (topography, vegetation, climate, context, local traditions, available resources, etc.), graph the sun path, and diagram the site constraints and views. From this information we write a clear, simple statement of the best strategy to meet needs and goals. We also apply Chris Alexander's pattern of leaving the "best spot" on the site alone; then building in the area most in need of repair.*

Build as Little as Possible
This might seem like an odd goal for architects, but reducing square footage saves resources, saves energy, and can also save money; building less can also allow for a greater level of detail within the space provided. We also look for opportunities to work with existing structures and improve them, both in their thermal and passive performance, and aesthetically.

Minimize Energy Dependence
The single largest impact over a building's lifetime is energy usage. Buildings should be able to heat and cool themselves and generate their own electricity. Passive heating and cooling are a good place to start: daylighting plus efficient systems reduce energy demands to a point where renewable sources can be integrated into the design, creating self-sufficient structures.

Maximize Resource Efficiency
Careful material specification yields considerable use of reused and recycled materials, plus resource-efficient building systems like strawbale and rammed earth. Getting these materials or systems into the project can require additional research or coordination with suppliers and, in some cases, sourcing or fabricating. In strawbale or earth construction, we provide information to building officials, sometimes conducting tests during construction.

Demonstrate the Beauty of Ecological Design
We strongly believe that for ecological design to take hold, it must be uplifting and inspire delight in the natural world. Ecology is the true basis of good design — in daylighting and rich materials, in buildings that naturally suit their site and climate.

< For the roof, Gladwyn d'Souza chose EcoStar Majestic Slate shingles. Made from 100 percent post-industrial waste rubber and plastic, they mimic the look of slate. Photos © 2005 Erik Kolderup.

* **A Pattern Language: Towns, Buildings, Construction,** by Christopher Alexander, Sara Ishikawa and Murray Silverstein, Oxford University Press. As relevant today as when it was first published in 1977, it's a seminal book on architecture and design, from the microlevel of single rooms to the macrolevel of whole communities.

Glossary

Adaptable building A building than can be readily remodeled or reconfigured to meet an occupant's or community's evolving needs.

Adaptive reuse Preserving and sometimes altering a building by changing its type of occupancy, such as converting a warehouse into lofts or an old church into a residence.

Bamboo A giant fast-growing grass with a hollow stem. In building design, bamboo is considered an environmentally friendly alternative to hardwood because it can be harvested every three to five years. Tongue-and-groove bamboo floor planks are available prefinished or unfinished, with a vertical or horizontal grain. Bamboo plywood and panels are also used for cabinetry and other interior furnishings and finishes.

Biodiesel A fuel derived from vegetable oils such as soybean oil or waste cooking oil from restaurants. Used primarily in diesel-powered vehicles but can also be substituted for home heating oil. It is environmentally preferable to conventional diesel because it is renewable, biodegradable, less polluting and has the potential to reduce our dependence on imported oil.

Brownfield A property, the expansion, redevelopment, or reuse of which may be complicated by the presence or potential presence of a hazardous substance, pollutant, or contaminant (as defined by the U.S. Environmental Protection Agency).

Building envelope A building's shell, including exterior walls, windows, doors, roof and the bottom floor.

Building paper Asphalt-impregnated paper used on roofs and exterior walls to help resist penetration of rain into the home.

Cellulose insulation Insulation made from wood fiber, primarily recycled newspaper, treated with nontoxic chemicals to retard fire, mold and insects. Loose-fill cellulose can be blown into attic spaces or packed into wall cavities. Damp-spray cellulose is a damp mix of cellulose and adhesives that is sprayed into wall cavities before hanging drywall.

Certified wood Wood certified by an independent third-party certification program to have been grown and harvested using environmentally responsible forestry practices.

Clerestory A window or row of windows placed high on a wall, often above the main roofline, used for introducing daylight into a room.

Daylighting The controlled use of natural light (as opposed to electric light) to illuminate a space. The goal is typically to create a stimulating, appealing environment while reducing energy use from electric lighting.

Deconstruction Disassembling rather than demolishing a building so that its components can be reused.

Design for disassembly Designing products or buildings so that at the end of their useful life they can be readily taken apart and their components reused, refurbished or recycled instead of landfilled or incinerated.

Dimensional lumber Wood that has been run through a mill and squared for use in framing the walls, floors and roofs of a building.

Dioxin A group of chemicals that are highly persistent in the environment and among the most toxic known. Dioxin is an unintentional by-product of many industrial processes involving chlorine. A potent human carcinogen, dioxin accumulates in animal fat and increases in concentration as it travels up the food chain.

Dogtrot A type of house common in the southeastern United States in the nineteenth century, characterized by two cabins or rooms connected by a central passageway, or dogtrot, that was open on two sides. A continuous gabled roof covered the cabins and dogtrot. The dogtrot provided shade and caught breezes to keep the home cool.

Double-pane (or double-glazed) window A window with two panes of glass separated by an airspace. Compared to single-glazed windows, double-glazed windows significantly reduce heat and sound transmission. Some double-glazed windows contain a gas such as argon or krypton in the air gap to provide additional insulation.

Dual-flush toilet A toilet designed to reduce water use, with two buttons or a specialized lever that allows the user to select a short or long flush.

Energy efficiency Using less electricity or fuel than a conventional technology to perform the same task.

Energy Star A program sponsored jointly by the U.S. Environmental Protection Agency and the U.S. Department of Energy that promotes energy-efficient products, homes and technologies for consumers and businesses. Energy Star–qualified products and new homes are typically 10 to 30 percent more efficient than their conventional counterparts.

Engineered wood Building products, including beams, framing studs, and floor and roof joists, made from wood fibers bound with adhesives. The wood typically comes from plantation-grown trees, thus reducing demand for old-growth trees. In general, engineered wood products result in less wood waste than solid sawn lumber products.

Fiber-cement siding An exterior siding product made from a blend of portland cement, sand, cellulose fiber and additives. It's typically sold as planks or panels, with a smooth or textured finish.

Fly ash A waste product from coal-fired electric power plants that can be used as a substitute for portland cement in some concrete mixtures. Portland cement manufacturing is an energy-intensive process, producing significant carbon dioxide (CO_2) emissions that contribute to global warming. Substituting fly ash for the portland cement in concrete reduces CO_2 emissions.

Footprint In architecture, the area of land covered by a building. (The term "ecological footprint," on the other hand, is used by environmentalists to indicate the number of acres of productive land necessary to support the resources a person consumes.)

Forest Stewardship Council (FSC) An international certification organization that has established voluntary environmental forest management standards. FSC accredits independent third-party organizations that monitor and certify the compliance of forestry operations with FSC standards. FSC-labeled wood products give consumers assurance that the wood comes from trees grown and harvested in an environmentally responsible manner.

Formaldehyde A colorless, pungent gas used in many glues, adhesives, preservatives and coatings. It also occurs naturally. Products and materials containing formaldehyde can offgas the chemical into the air (products containing urea formaldehyde typically offgas at much higher levels than products containing phenol formaldehyde). According to the U.S. Environmental Protection Agency, exposure to formaldehyde may cause allergic reactions, respiratory problems or cancer in humans.

FSC See Forest Stewardship Council.

Global warming The long-term warming of the planet caused by heat being trapped in the lower atmosphere by greenhouse gases. These gases are being emitted primarily as a result of human activities, including burning fossil fuels.

Glulam Abbreviation of "glued laminated" timber. An engineered wood product consisting of thin layers of wood, usually less than two inches thick, bound with an adhesive and formed into structural beams that can be used instead of solid sawn lumber.

Green building Building practices that use energy, water and other resources wisely so that present and future generations can live well without needlessly damaging the environment. Also called sustainable, eco-friendly or environmentally responsible building.

Green Label A voluntary testing and labeling program developed by a trade association, the Carpet and Rug Institute, to identify carpets, rugs, adhesives and carpet cushions that emit lower levels of indoor air pollutants compared to conventional products.

Green roof A roof that has a layer of soil or other growing medium on top of a waterproofing membrane. May be planted with sedum, grasses, wildflowers or other ground cover. Also known as a living, eco or vegetated roof.

Heat island effect The tendency of large areas of roofs, asphalt, concrete and paved surfaces to absorb heat, making urban areas considerably hotter than nearby rural areas.

Heat loss The decrease of heat in a space as a result of heat escaping through the building's walls, windows, roof and other building envelope components.

Heat-recovery ventilation A heat recovery ventilation system (also known as an air-to-air heat exchanger) saves energy by capturing heat from indoor air that's about to be vented from a home and transferring that heat to fresh air that's being drawn in from the outside.

High performance A building or building component designed to be more energy or resource efficient, healthy and comfortable than a conventional building or building component.

Indoor air quality The level of air pollutants inside a building. Indoor air pollution sources include tobacco and wood smoke; certain building materials and furnishings; certain cleaning, maintenance and personal care products; dust mites; pet dander; mold; radon; pesticides; and outdoor air pollution. Inadequate ventilation and high humidity levels can also contribute to indoor air-quality problems.

Infill development Building on empty or underutilized lots in cities or older suburban areas instead of building in a previously undeveloped area. Reduces pressure to develop agricultural lands and wildlands.

Insulated concrete form (ICF) Plastic foam shaped into hollow blocks, panels or planks and used as a form to create a concrete wall. After positioning the foam forms, rebar is typically inserted into the cavities to reinforce the walls, and then concrete is poured in. Once the concrete cures, the foam remains in place to insulate the walls. Exterior siding and interior wall finishes are attached to the ICFs.

Insulation A material that has a high resistance to heat flow. Used to keep a home comfortable and reduce the energy needed to heat and cool the home.

Kilowatt (kW) A unit of electrical power equal to 1,000 watts.

Lead-based paint Lead was a common additive to oil-based paints before 1978, and it can pose a serious health risk, particularly for babies and children, if lead-based paint chips are ingested or lead-based paint dust is inhaled. According to the U.S. Environmental Protection Agency, lead-based paint remains a serious childhood health hazard.

LEED Green Building Rating System A voluntary, consensus-based national standard for high-performance, sustainable buildings. Developed and administered by the U.S. Green Building Council.

Low-e (low-emissivity) window A window with a special coating that allows daylight to enter a building but reduces the flow of heat. The appropriate type of low-e glazing for a home will depend on the climate and the window's orientation.

Material recovery facility (MRF) Facility where refuse from municipal and commercial haulers is sorted to retrieve recyclable materials, diverting that material from landfill disposal.

Medium-density fiberboard (MDF) A composite board made of sawmill waste bound with urea formaldehyde or other synthetic resins. Similar to particleboard but made with smaller wood particles so it mills cleanly. Used in place of wood boards for cabinets, furniture, molding and the like. Medite II, an MDF product made by Sierra Pine, is made without formaldehyde.

Mixed-use development A building or site that combines several types of commercial uses (retail, office, restaurants, etc.) with housing, rather than segregating commercial and residential uses into separate zones or neighborhoods.

Native vegetation Plants that are indigenous to a particular area, as opposed to occurring there due to human intervention. Landscaping with native plants reduces or eliminates the need for water, fertilizers and pesticides; provides shelter and food for wildlife; and promotes biodiversity.

Natural cooling Cooling a building through passive means rather than mechanical systems such as air-conditioning. Natural cooling strategies include shading, cross ventilation and the use of thermal mass to moderate temperatures inside a space.

Natural oil finish Wood finish made from vegetable oils and waxes, for flooring, trim, furniture and other wood products.

Natural ventilation The introduction of outside air into a building using passive means such as open windows and cross ventilation, rather than using mechanical systems such as air conditioners, heating systems or fans.

Net metering A billing agreement available in many states that allows small power producers, such as homeowners with photovoltaic systems, to feed directly to the utility grid any electricity they generate in excess of their current demand. This causes the electricity meter to spin backwards, essentially selling that power back to the utility system at retail price.

Offgas The release of vapors from a material through the process of evaporation or chemical decomposition. Many building products, furnishings, floor and wall coverings and other products brought into the home offgas formaldehyde, volatile organic compounds (VOCs) or other potentially troublesome chemicals.

Old-growth tree A tree that has been growing for approximately 200 years or longer.

Oriented strand board (OSB) An engineered wood panel made from strands of wood arranged in crisscrossing layers and bound with an adhesive. In homes, used for subflooring and sheathing.

Passive solar design A building specifically designed to collect and store the sun's heat, and release that heat into the interior spaces to help warm the rooms naturally. Depending on the design and climate, passive solar heating can be the sole source of heat for the building or can be supplemented with a heating system.

Permeable paving Paving material that allows rainwater to seep into the soil, thereby reducing the amount of rainwater that the municipal water treatment system must handle.

Photovoltaic (PV) cell A material that converts sunlight directly into electricity.

PISÉ An acronym for pneumatically impacted stabilized earth. Pioneered by David Easton of Rammed Earth Works in Napa, California, PISE is a system of building thick earthen walls using a high-pressure air hose to spray a damp soil mix against one-sided formwork.

Plaster veneer Typically, one or two coats of wet plaster thinly applied (1/8 inch) over a type of gypsum wall board called blueboard, creating a much harder finish than drywall alone. Less expensive and less labor-intensive than old-fashioned lath-and-plaster walls, plaster veneer can be left in its natural off-white state, colorant can be added to the plaster, or it can be painted.

Polycarbonate A lightweight, durable, shatter-resistant plastic used in thousands of everyday products; in the building industry, polycarbonate sheets are used for greenhouses, sunrooms, roofs and other applications where light transmission, strength and durability are desirable.

Polyisocyanurate insulation A rigid material consisting of expanded foam, often faced with foil. Widely used in the construction industry to insulate buildings. Typical thicknesses range from 1/2 inch to 4 inches.

Polyvinyl chloride Also known as vinyl or PVC. A family of plastics, derived from vinyl chloride, with a wide range of forms and uses. PVC is used extensively in building products, consumer goods and industrial applications. There has been considerable debate about the environmental impacts related to PVC manufacturing and the eventual disposal of products made from PVC. Some groups have called for phasing out PVC production or limiting its use.

Portland cement A component of concrete, made from limestone, sand and clay that is fired at an intense heat in a kiln.

Post-consumer recycled content Materials that have been used and discarded by a consumer and are then reprocessed as raw material for a new product. Post-consumer recycled content has been diverted from landfills or incinerators, usually as part of residential or commercial recycling programs, and is environmentally preferable to post-industrial recycled content.

Post-industrial (or pre-consumer) recycled content Waste material from a manufacturer or processor, including scrap, trimmings, and overruns, used as the raw material to make a new product. For most manufacturers, the reuse of post-industrial waste is a normal part of doing business; this type of waste is not likely to end up in landfills.

Prefab Building components or whole buildings manufactured at a factory and transported to the building site for installation, as opposed to conventional buildings constructed at the site.

Pressure-treated wood Wood treated with chemicals to prevent moisture decay, typically used in places where the wood might come into contact with soil.

PVC See polyvinyl chloride.

Radiant-floor heating system A heating system in which warm water circulates through tubes embedded in a concrete floor slab or attached to the subflooring beneath a hardwood floor. The floor absorbs heat from the tubes and slowly releases it to the room, providing a comfortable, quiet, gentle warmth that doesn't stir dust or create drafts. While water is the most frequent heat source, some radiant-floor systems use electricity or hot air.

Rainwater harvesting Collecting rainwater from a catchment area such as a roof and storing it in cisterns or other containers to use for watering a yard or garden, or for other purposes.

Rammed-earth construction Buildings, walls or other structures made from a moist mix of earth, sand and cement tamped or "rammed" into temporary forms. The compressed earthen walls cure to a rock-like hardness.

Reclaimed material A material that's put to a new beneficial use after it is no longer needed for its original use, such as wood removed from an abandoned building and used to construct a new building.

Recycling Taking a material that would otherwise become waste and processing it into raw material for a new product.

Renewable energy Energy generated from replenishable resources, such as sunlight, wind and agricultural products.

Renewable resource A material that can be replenished in a relatively short period of time after it is harvested or used.

R-value A measure of a material's resistance to the passage of heat through it. The higher the R-value, the more effective the material is as insulation.

SEER Seasonal Energy Efficiency Ratio. Indicates an air conditioner's energy efficiency. The higher the SEER, the more efficient the air conditioner.

Sinker logs Cut logs that sank to river bottoms during logging operations. Also known as deadhead. Salvage operations retrieve high-quality sinker logs, typically from old-growth trees, for use in building construction.

Skylight A translucent or transparent window set into a roof to allow daylight into a building.

Smart growth A community planning movement that offers an alternative to unchecked, sprawling development. It advocates protecting open space and farmland, preserving natural and cultural resources, revitalizing inner cities and inner suburbs, and creating communities that are livable and affordable.

Solar collector A device used to capture solar energy to heat water.

Solar electricity Electricity generated from sunlight. Also called photovoltaic or PV power.

Solar orientation The relationship of a building, or a window or other building component, to compass direction and consequently to the sun's position. Careful solar orientation is a fundamental aspect of passive solar design and daylighting.

Sprawl The spread of low-density, dispersed residential and commercial development outside of compact cities, towns and villages.

Sprayed-earth construction Erecting walls using a high-pressure hose to spray a moist mix of earth, sand and cement against one-sided formwork.

Stack ventilation Planned ventilation design that naturally cools a home by taking advantage of the high- and low-pressure zones created by the rising of warm air. An exit vent near the top of the house, sometimes in a tower, draws warm air out of the building, while fresh cool air is pulled in through vents located at lower levels in the home.

Storm-felled trees Trees that fell naturally on private or municipal property, as opposed to trees deliberately logged.

Stormwater runoff Water that flows off of buildings and paved surfaces and over land during a rainstorm.

Strawbale construction A construction method that uses straw bales to form walls. The bales can be load-bearing, meaning that they carry some or all of the roof's weight. More commonly, however, the bales are stacked within a structural framework to provide superior insulation. Straw is an agricultural waste product—it's what's left after harvesting rice, wheat, barley and other grains.

Strawboard A panel product made primarily from compressed straw, an agricultural waste product. Typically made without formaldehyde binders. Used for cabinet boxes, floor underlayment, furniture, paneling and other interior applications.

Structural insulating panel (SIP) An alternative to framing with wood studs and joists. SIPs can be used to build well-insulated floors, walls and roofs. They are prefabricated panels that typically consist of rigid foam insulation sandwiched between two panels of oriented strand board or plywood.

Studs Lumber used for vertical framing in a house.

Sustainability Meeting the needs of the present without compromising the ability of future generations to meet their own needs (as defined by the World Commission on the Environment and Development).

Sustainably harvested Plants (typically trees) managed and harvested carefully to protect habitats, biodiversity, water quality and the rights of indigenous people who depend on the land.

Swale A shallow depression or hollow in the ground used to slow the flow of stormwater off a property.

Tankless water heater A water heater that saves energy by heating water as it is needed, rather than storing hot water in a tank. Also known as an instantaneous or demand water heater.

Thermal bridge A highly conductive material within a building envelope, such as a steel-framing member, that allows heat to bypass the insulation.

Thermal mass The ability of a material to absorb and retain heat. Materials with a high thermal mass, such as rocks, earth and concrete, have the capacity to absorb heat during the day and release it when temperatures cool.

Toxic Capable of adversely affecting organisms.

Trombe wall A low-tech means of collecting heat from the sun and transferring it into a space. Typically consists of a thick masonry wall coated with a dark material and faced with a layer of glass. A small airspace separates the glass from the wall. Heat from the sun passes through the glass, is absorbed by the dark surface, and slowly conducted to the interior of the wall.

Truss A structural framework for supporting roofs or floors. Prefabricated trusses are shipped to the building site ready to install, and are typically fashioned of small pieces of wood joined with metal plates into a triangulated form. They use less wood, and save time and money compared to site-built rafters and joists.

Truth window An opening in a wall surface that reveals the components within the wall.

Universal design An approach to designing a product or a building to make it more easily usable by people of all ages and diverse physical abilities.

U.S. Green Building Council A voluntary coalition of building industry professionals working to promote buildings that are environmentally responsible, profitable and healthy places to live and work. Administers the LEED Green Building Rating System.

Vapor barrier A material used in certain climates to reduce or stop the flow of moisture in vapor form. Typically made of plastic or foil sheeting or treated kraft paper, vapor barriers are sometimes attached to insulation batts or rigid insulation.

Ventilation The process of bringing outside air into an indoor space, by natural or mechanical means.

Vinyl See polyvinyl chloride.

Visible transmittance Indicates the amount of visible light transmitted through a window. The higher the visible transmittance, the more light is transmitted.

Volatile organic compound (VOC) A class of organic chemicals that readily release gaseous vapors at room temperature. VOCs occur naturally in many materials, and can also be manufactured and added to materials and products. VOCs are released ("offgassed") into a home by common furnishings and building materials, including many types of particleboard, paint, solvents, carpets and synthetic fabrics. Exposure to VOCs can cause symptoms ranging from short-term nausea, eye irritation and headaches to more severe, longer-lasting effects.

Wheatboard See strawboard.

References

© 2005 Erik Kolderup

Bottle House, Rhyolite, Nevada.

Abrams, John. *The Company We Keep: Reinventing Small Business for People, Community, and Place*. White River Junction, VT: Chelsea Green Publishing Co., 2005.

Alexander, Christopher, Sara Ishikawa and Murray Silverstein. *A Pattern Language: Towns, Buildings, Construction*. Oxford University Press, 1977.

Burkhart, Bryan, and Allison Arieff. *Prefab*. Salt Lake City, UT: Gibbs Smith, Publisher, 2002.

Corson, Jennifer. *The Resourceful Renovator: A Gallery of Ideas for Reusing Building Materials*. White River Junction, VT: Chelsea Green Publishing Co., 2000.

Dwell. San Francisco. www.dwellmag.com.

Environmental Building News. Brattleboro, VT: BuildingGreen, Inc. www.buildinggreen.com.

Falk, Robert H., and G. Bradley Guy. *Directory of Wood-Framed Building Deconstruction and Reused Building Materials Companies*. Madison, WI: U.S. Department of Agriculture, Forest Service, Forest Products Laboratory. Publication no. FPL-GTR-150, 2004.

King, Bruce. *Buildings of Earth and Straw: Structural Design for Rammed Earth and Straw Bale Architecture*. Sausalito, CA: Ecological Design Press (Distributed by Chelsea Green Publishing Co., White River Junction, VT), 1997.

Hayden, Dolores. *A Field Guide to Sprawl*. New York: W. W. Norton & Company, 2004.

Lilienfeld, Robert. *Use Less Stuff: Environmental Solutions for Who We Really Are*. New York: Ballantine Books, 1998.

McDonough, William, and Michael Braungart. *Cradle to Cradle: Remaking the Way We Make Things*. New York: North Point Press, 2002.

Rathje, William, and Cullen Murphy. *Rubbish! The Archaeology of Garbage*. Tucson: University of Arizona Press, 2001.

Roberts, Jennifer. *Good Green Homes: Creating Better Homes for a Healthier Planet*. Salt Lake City, UT: Gibbs Smith, Publisher, 2003.

Ruskin, John. *The Seven Lamps of Architecture*. Rev. ed. New York: Dover Publications, 1989 (originally published 1849).

Siegal, Jennifer. *Mobile: The Art of Portable Architecture*. Princeton Architectural Press, 2002.

Steen, Athena and Bill. *The Beauty of Straw Bale Homes*. White River Junction, VT: Chelsea Green Publishing Co., 2000.

Stegner, Wallace. "The Town Dump." *Atlantic Monthly*. Oct. 1959, vol. 204, no. 4.

Thoreau, Henry David. *Walden*. Boston, MA: Houghton Mifflin, 1995.

Wanek, Catherine. *The New Strawbale Home*. Salt Lake City, UT: Gibbs Smith, Publisher, 2003.

Resources

The programs, products and resources listed in this resource section and throughout this book are provided for informational purposes only and are not endorsed by the author or Gibbs Smith, Publisher.

Deconstruction & House Moving

Deconstruction Institute, www.deconstructioninstitute.com
Directory of Wood-Framed Building Deconstruction and Reused Building Materials Companies
        published by the USDA's Forest Products Laboratory (www.treesearch.fs.fed.us)
International Association of Structural Movers, www.iasm.org

Energy Efficiency

Alliance to Save Energy, www.ase.org
American Council for an Energy-Efficient Economy, www.aceee.org
Efficient Windows Collaborative, www.efficientwindows.org
Home Energy magazine, www.homeenergy.org
Rocky Mountain Institute, www.rmi.org
U.S. Department of Energy's Building America program,
        www.eere.energy.gov/buildings/building_america
U.S. Environmental Protection Agency and U.S. Department of Energy's
        ENERGY STAR program, www.energystar.gov

^
In Vermont, a railing of old skis.

© 2005 Karl Wanaselja

Green Building

GENERAL GREEN BUILDING RESOURCES

Architects, Designers and Planners for Social Responsibility, www.adpsr.org
Ecological Building Network, www.ecobuildnetwork.org
BuildingGreen, Inc., and *Environmental Building News,* www.buildinggreen.com
U.S. Green Building Council, usgbc.org

GREEN HOME PROGRAMS & RESOURCES

Listed here are green home programs that have particularly good information online for homeowners who are remodeling or building a new home. In addition, many regional home-builders associations sponsor green certification programs for professional builders; the U.S. Green Building Council lists these programs in the LEED for Homes section of their Web site (www.usgbc.org).

PROGRAM	STATE	WEB
Build It Green	CA	www.build-green.org
Green Building in Alameda County	CA	www.BuildGreenNow.org
GreenHome NYC	NY	www.greenhomenyc.org
Earth Advantage	OR	www.earthadvantage.com
City of Portland's G/Rated program	OR	www.green-rated.org
Austin Energy Green Building Program	TX	www.ci.austin.tx.us/greenbuilder
City of Seattle green home remodeling resources	WA	www.ci.seattle.wa.us/sustainablebuilding

GREEN PRODUCT GUIDES & RESOURCE DIRECTORIES

Build It Green Materials Database, www.build-green.org/guide
Building Concerns Regional Resource Directories, www.buildingconcerns.com
GreenHomeGuide, Northern California, www.greenhomeguide.com
Green Seal, www.greenseal.org
GreenSpec Directory, www.buildinggreen.com
Northwest Green Directory, www.nwgreendirectory.com

GREEN BUILDING PRODUCTS STORES

Company	City	State	Phone	Web
Real Goods	Hopland	CA	707.744.2100	www.realgoods.com
Green Fusion Design Center	San Anselmo	CA	415.454.0174	www.greenfusiondesigncenter.com
Eco Design Resources	San Carlos	CA	650.591.1123	www.ecodesignresources.com
Building for Health Materials Center	Carbondale	CO	800.292.4838	www.buildingforhealth.com
Environmental Construction Outfitters	Bronx	NY	800.238.5008	www.environproducts.com
Environmental Building Supplies	Portland	OR	503.222.3881	www.ecohaus.com
Environmental Home Center	Seattle	WA	800.281.9785	www.environmentalhomecenter.com

MISCELLANEOUS GREEN LIVING RESOURCES

Center for the New American Dream, promotes responsible consumerism, www.newdream.org
Earth Pledge, green roofs and other sustainability initiatives, www.earthpledge.org
Littlearth, recycled fashion accessories from old license plates, www.littlearth.com
Gaiam, online store, www.gaiam.com
Green Home, online store, www.greenhome.com
GreenSage, online store, www.greensage.com
Natural Home & Garden magazine, www.naturalhomemagazine.com

HEALTHY BUILDING & INDOOR AIR QUALITY

AFM Safecoat zero-VOC paints and finishes, www.afmsafecoat.com
American Lung Association, www.healthhouse.org
Blue Vinyl, www.bluevinyl.org
Healthy Building Network, www.healthybuilding.net
Greenpeace, www.greenpeace.org
My House Is Your House, www.myhouseisyourhouse.org
U.S. Environmental Protection Agency, www.epa.gov
   Brownfields remediation: www.epa.gov/brownfields
   Indoor air quality: www.epa.gov/iaq
   Lead: www.epa.gov/lead

RENEWABLE ENERGY

American Solar Energy Society, www.ases.org
Solar Living Institute, www.solarliving.org

© 2005 Karl Wanaselja

^
Flattened cans used for siding in Nevada.

SALVAGED MATERIALS

ONLINE NETWORKS & EXCHANGES OF USED GOODS

Company	Web	Company	Web
California Materials Exchange	www.ciwmb.ca.gov/calmax	Freecycle	www.freecycle.org
Craigslist	www.craigslist.org	Green Guide Salvaged Building Materials Exchange	www.greenguide.com
eBay	www.ebay.com	Vermont Business Materials Exchange	www.vbmex.net

RECLAIMED LUMBER, FLOORING & MILLWORK

Company	City	State	Phone	Web
James & Company	Collinsville	AL	256.997.0703	www.jamesandcompany.com
Pacific Heritage Wood	El Granada	CA	877.728.9231	www.phwood.com
TerraMai	McCloud	CA	800.220.9062	www.terramai.com
Crossroads Recycled Lumber	North Fork	CA	888.842.3201	www.crossroadslumber.com
Restoration Timber	San Anselmo	CA	888-563-9663	www.restorationtimber.com
Black's Farmwood	San Rafael	CA	877.321.WOOD	www.blacksfarmwood.com
EcoTimber	San Rafael	CA	415.258.8454	www.ecotimber.com
Vintage Timberworks	Temecula	CA	951.695.1003	www.vintagetimber.com
Recycled Lumberworks	Ukiah	CA	707.462.2567	www.oldwoodguy.com
Old Grain Reclaimed Wood Specialists	Carbondale	CO	877.704.9745	www.oldgrain.com
A Reclaimed Lumber Co.	Madison	CT	203.214.9705	www.woodwood.com
Old Wood Workshop	Pomfret Center	CT	860.974.3622	www.oldwoodworkshop.com
Pinetree Builders	Fort Lauderdale	FL	800.383.5598	www.pinetreebuilders.com
Goodwin Heart Pine Company	Micanopy	FL	800.336.3118	www.heartpine.com
Vintage Lumber Sales	Gay	GA	706.538.0180	www.vintagelumbersales.com
Trestlewood	Blackfoot	ID	877.375.2779	www.trestlewood.com
Carlson's Barnwood Co.	Cambridge	IL	309.522.5550	www.carlsonsbarnwood.com
Whiskey Wood	Hartford	KY	270.298.0084	www.whiskeywood.com
Longleaf Lumber	Cambridge	MA	866.OLD.FLOOR	www.longleaflumber.com
Duluth Timber Co.	Duluth	MN	218.727.2145	www.duluthtimber.com
Big Timberworks	Gallatin Gateway	MT	406.763.4639	www.bigtimberworks.com
Vintage Beams & Timbers, Inc.	Sylva	NC	828.586.0755	www.vintagebeamsandtimbers.com
CitiLog	Pittstown	NJ	877.CITY LOG	www.citilogs.com
Big Wood	East Bethany	NY	800.452.8251	www.big-wood.net
Pioneer Millworks	Farmington	NY	800.951.9663	www.pioneermillworks.com
Antique Woods & Colonial Restorations	Gouverneur	NY	888.261.4284	www.vintagewoods.com
Craftmark Reclaimed Wood	McMinnville	OR	503.472.6929	www.craftmarkinc.com
Endura Wood Products	Portland	OR	503.233.7090	www.endurawood.com
The Barnwood Connection	Barto	PA	610.845.3101	www.barnwoodconnection.com
The Woods Company, Inc.	Chambersburg	PA	888.548.7609	www.thewoodscompany.com
Conklin's Authentic Antique Barnwood	Susquehanna	PA	570.465.3832	www.conklinsbarnwood.com
Aged Woods	York	PA	800.233.9307	www.agedwoods.com

Vintage Material Supply Co.	Austin	TX	512.386.6404	www.vintagematerialsupply.com
What Its Worth, Inc.	Austin	TX	512.328.8837	www.wiwpine.com
Trestlewood	Lindon	UT	877.375.2779	www.trestlewood.com
Antiquus Wood Products	Salt Lake City	UT	800.852.9224	www.antiquuswood.com
Antique Building Products, Inc.	Amherst	VA	800.653.7463	www.antiquebuildingproducts.com
Shenandoah Valley Reclaimed Lumber	Harrisonburg	VA	540.896.7600	www.svreclaimedlumber.com
E. T. Moore, Inc.	Richmond	VA	804.231.1823	www.etmoore.com
Mountain Lumber	Ruckersville	VA	800.445.2671	www.mountainlumber.com
Appalachian Woods	Stuarts Draft	VA	800.333.7610	www.appalachianwoods.com
Retech Wood Products	Forks	WA	360.374.4141	www.retechwoodproducts.com
Windfall Lumber Products	Olympia	WA	360.352.2250	www.windfalllumber.com
Urban Hardwoods	Seattle	WA	206.766.8199	www.urbanhardwoods.com
R. W. Rhine, Inc.	Tacoma	WA	800.963.8270	www.rwrhine.com
Timeless Timber	Ashland	WI	888.OLD.LOGS	www.timelesstimber.com
Vintage Log and Lumber	Alderson	WV	877.OLD.LOGS	www.vintagelog.com

SALVAGE YARDS, REUSE STORES & ARCHITECTURAL SALVAGE SHOPS

Company	City	State	Phone	Web
Habitat for Humanity ReStores	Nationwide			www.habitat.org/env/restores.aspx
The Reuse People	Alameda	CA	510.522.2722	www.thereusepeople.org
Ohmega Salvage	Berkeley	CA	510.204.0767	www.ohmegasalvage.com
Urban Ore	Berkeley	CA	510.841.7283	N/A
Beyond Waste	Cotati	CA	707.792.2555	www.beyondwaste.com
Whole House Building Supply & Salvage	East Palo Alto	CA	650.328.8731	www.driftwoodsalvage.com
Santa Fe Wrecking Co.	Los Angeles	CA	213.623.3119	www.santafewrecking.com
Architectural Detail	Pasadena	CA	626.844.6670	www.pasadenasalvage.com
Building Resources	San Francisco	CA	415.285.7814	www.buildingresources.org
Caldwell's	San Francisco	CA	415.550.6777	www.caldwell-bldg-salvage.com
Garbage Reincarnation	Santa Rosa	CA	707.795.1395	www.garbage.org
ReSource	Boulder	CO	303.419.5418	www.resource2k.org
United House Wrecking	Stamford	CT	203.348.5371	www.united-antiques.com
The Back Doors Warehouse	Washington	DC	202.265.0587	www.thebrassknob.com
Florida Victorian Architectural Antiques	DeLand	FL	386.734.9300	www.floridavictorian.com
American Salvage	Miami	FL	305.691.7001	www.americansalvage.com
Sarasota Architectural Salvage	Sarasota	FL	941.362.0803	www.sarasotasalvage.com
Pinch of the Past	Savannah	GA	912.232.5563	www.pinchofthepast.com
Gavin Historical Bricks	Iowa City	IA	319.354.5251	www.historicalbricks.com
Salvage Barn	Iowa City	IA	800.541.8656	www.ic-fhp.org/salvagebarn.html
Building Material Thrift Store	Hailey	ID	208.788.0014	www.woodriverlandtrust.org/store/store.html
Salvage One	Chicago	IL	312.733.0098	www.salvageone.com
Tim & Avi's Salvage Store	Indianapolis	IN	317.925.6071	www.architecturalantiques.net
White River Architectural Salvage	Indianapolis	IN	800.262.3389	www.whiteriversalvage.com

Carrollton Lumber & Wrecking Co.	New Orleans	LA	504.861.3681	www.carrolltonlumber.com
Nor'East Architectural Antiques	Amesbury	MA	978.834.9088	www.noreast1.com
Building Materials Resource Center	Boston	MA	617.442.8917	www.bostonbmrc.org
Olde Bostonian Architectural Antiques	Dorchester	MA	617.282.9300	www.oldbostonian.com
The Loading Dock	Baltimore	MD	410.728.DOCK	www.loadingdock.org
Maine Housing & Building Materials Exchange	Gray	ME	207.657.2957	www.mainebme.org
Old House Parts	Kennebunk	ME	207.985.1999	www.oldhouseparts.com
Portland Architectural Salvage	Portland	ME	207.780.0634	www.portlandsalvage.com
The Reuse Center	Ann Arbor	MI	734.662.6288	www.recycleannarbor.org/reuse/reuse.html
City Salvage Antiques	Minneapolis	MN	612.627.9107	www.citysalvage.com
Green Institute	Minneapolis	MN	612.724.2608	www.greeninstitute.org
North Shore Architectural Antiques	Two Harbors	MN	218.834.0018	www.north-shore-architectural-antiques.com
Preservation Hall	Weaverville	NC	828.645.1047	www.preservation-hall.com
Recycling the Past	Barnegat	NJ	609.660.9790	www.recyclingthepast.com
Renovators Resource	Halifax	Nova Scotia	902.429.3889	www.renovators-resource.com
Significant Elements	Ithaca	NY	607.277.3450	www.significantelements.org
Demolition Depot	New York	NY	212.860.1138	www.demolitiondepot.com
Olde Good Things	New York	NY	212.989.8401	www.oldegoodthings.com
ReHouse	Rochester region	NY	585.872.1450	www.rehouseny.com
BRING Recycling	Eugene	OR	541.746.3023	www.bringrecycling.org
The Rebuilding Center	Portland	OR	503.331.1877	www.rebuildingcenter.org
Construction Junction	Pittsburgh	PA	412.243.5025	www.constructionjunction.org
Olde Good Things	Scranton	PA	570.341.7668	www.oldegoodthings.com
Discount Home Warehouse	Dallas	TX	214.631.2755	www.dhwsalvage.com
The Emporium	Houston	TX	800.528.3808	www.the-emporium.com
Caravati's	Richmond	VA	804.232.4175	www.recentruins.com
Black Dog Salvage	Roanoke	VA	540.343.6200	www.blackdogsalvage.com
Architectural Salvage Warehouse	Burlington	VT	802.658.5011	www.greatsalvage.com
Waste Not, Want Not	Port Townsend	WA	360.379.6838	www.wastenot-recycle.com
Earthwise	Seattle	WA	206.624.4510	www.earthwise-salvage.com
Second Use Building Materials	Seattle	WA	206.763.6929	www.seconduse.com

STRAW BUILDING & PRODUCTS

California Straw Building Association (CASBA), www.strawbuilding.org
Environ Biocomposites panel products made of agricultural waste and recycled materials. www.environbiocomposites.com
The Last Straw: The International Journal of Straw Bale and Natural Building, www.thelaststraw.org
PrimeBoard straw-based particleboard, www.primeboard.com
Woodstalk wheatboard panels, www.dow.com/bioprod

SUSTAINABLE FORESTRY RESOURCES

Forest Certification Resource Center, www.certifiedwood.org
Forest Stewardship Council, www.fsc.org
Natural Resources Defense Council, www.nrdc.org
Rainforest Alliance, www.rainforest-alliance.org
SmartWood, www.smartwood.org

Thanks

© 2005 Karl Wanaselja

Earth Ship under construction, New Mexico.

I'm fortunate to be doing work that I love and that brings me into the circles of so many creative, caring people.

I'm particularly grateful to David Arkin and Anni Tilt of Arkin Tilt Architects. They came up with the original concept for *Redux,* and lured me into the project when it became clear that they couldn't put their thriving architectural practice on hold in order to write a book. This book is not the same book David and Anni would have written, but I'm delighted that they remained involved in the project, providing insight and inspiration. I look forward to someday reading the books they will write.

I'm also extremely grateful to Cate Leger and Karl Wanaselja of Leger Wanaselja Architecture. Early on they sat down with me, David, Anni and Gibbs Smith to hash out the ideas that turned into this book. Throughout the process they remained remarkably generous with their time and talents, as well as with their personal photos of cool junk.

Warm thanks also to Gibbs Smith, who first approached me a few years back about doing a book about mud architecture. When I told him mud wasn't my thing, he wanted to know what my thing was. That conversation led to our first book together, *Good Green Homes,* and from there to *Redux.* To Suzanne Taylor, Madge Baird, Alison Einerson and the rest of the Gibbs Smith, Publisher, team who bring beautiful books into the world: thank you.

I would also like to thank the folks who took time to critique an early draft of this book: Scott Adler, David Arkin, Janis Brewer, Maria Hekker, Erik Kolderup, Cate Leger, Mark Roberts, Anni Tilt and Karl Wanaselja. Their insights and fresh perspectives were immeasurably helpful; any gaffes that remain are entirely my own doing.

Hundreds of people have sent me information about green homes, furniture made from salvaged goods, and eco-friendly products. There are too many of you to thank personally here, but I want you to know that your ideas and enthusiasm inspired me and helped shape this book.

Many thanks to the talented photographers who contributed to *Redux,* including Eric Laignel, Randi Baird, Brian Vanden Brink, Linda Svendsen, Cesar Rubio, Laurie Lambrecht, Kristopher Grunert, Undine Pröhl, Benny Chan, Edward Caldwell, John Christenson, Robert Meier and J. D. Peterson.

I'm particularly grateful to the people who took the time to show me their homes, track down images and information, or provide other invaluable assistance. In particular, I'd like to thank Brian Roberts, Ken Wilson, Sally Wilson, John Abrams, Betsy Smith, Donna Schumacher, Suzanne Jones, Rob Elia (and Rob's parents who babysat one-month-old Dean while we photographed the house!), Sarah Hoffmann, Jason McLennan, Marcia Stuermer, Heather Tremain, Carla Weinberg, Reuben Schwartz, Carl Scheidenhelm, Ann Schuessler, Brad Guy, Ted Reiff, Doug Farr, Elizabeth Lindau, Benton Brown, Susan Boyle, Jennifer Siegal, Suzanne Johnson, Rick Walters, Wynne Yelland, Paul Neseth, Judith Helfand, Henry Siegel and Kyra, Gladwyn d'Souza, Martina de la Torre, Richard Parker, Michael O'Brien and Chris Hammer. I'd also like to express my appreciation for the Green Building in Alameda County program, in particular Ann Ludwig, Karen Kho, Meri Soll and Wendy Sommer, whose work is transforming the way that homes are being built in the San Francisco Bay Area and beyond.

Thanks also to my father, Jerry Roberts, a consummate DIYer with a creative flair. As a kid I was astonished by how much time he could spend browsing in Rickels hardware store in Nanuet, New York; now I get it.

Finally, to Erik: with every heartbeat I thank you for being by my side on this amazing journey.